Believing God addresses one of the most significant problems in the church today: We do not take the Bible seriously. Specifically, in regard to God's amazing promises, we tend to believe only those that seem logical to us. R. C. Sproul Jr. helps us see that in Christ Jesus all of God's promises are "Yes" and are meant to be believed and relied upon. This book will stimulate your faith.

—JERRY BRIDGES
Bible teacher, conference speaker,
Author, *The Pursuit of Holiness*
and other titles

Most of us only scratch the surface of what it means to believe God. We say we "take Him at His Word," but do we? The book you hold in your hands presents the supreme promises of God we fight to hold on to, and what each one conveys about our awesome Creator and Redeemer. Thank you, R. C. Jr., for showing us how to enter—how to believe—the promises of God and truly live.

—JONI EARECKSON TADA
Founder, Joni and Friends
International Disability Center
Agoura Hills, California

Many years ago, I first heard the cute catchphrase "Some people are just sitting on the premises instead of standing on the promises." As a fired-up young Christian, I was quite sure it didn't apply to me. More than fifty years later, *Believing God* has challenged me to have a reality check. R. C. Sproul Jr.'s excellent approach to twelve key biblical promises achieves the combination of being both forensic and pastoral, clinical and tender, surgical and sympathetic. Read it carefully, apply it diligently—then be sure to pass it on to somebody else. I predict it will do a power of good.

—JOHN BLANCHARD
Preacher, teacher, and apologist
Author, *Does God Believe in Atheists?*

This book is rich provision for all of us who have cried out, "Lord, I believe. Help me in my unbelief." R. C. Jr. has marshaled the hope of faith for a host of our recurring doubts—that we might be tossed to and fro no longer.

—GEORGE GRANT
Pastor, Parish Presbyterian Church,
Franklin, Tennessee
Founder, King's Meadow Study Center

BELIEVING GOD

TWELVE BIBLICAL PROMISES CHRISTIANS STRUGGLE TO ACCEPT

R. C. SPROUL JR.

Reformation Trust

PUBLISHING

A DIVISION OF LIGONIER MINISTRIES • ORLANDO, FLORIDA

Believing God: *Twelve Biblical Promises Christians Struggle to Accept*
© 2009 by R. C. Sproul Jr.
Published by Reformation Trust
a division of Ligonier Ministries
400 Technology Park, Lake Mary, FL 32746
www.Ligonier.org www.ReformationTrust.com

Printed in the United States of America

Cover design: Kirk DouPonce, www.DogEaredDesign.com
Interior design and typeset: Katherine Lloyd, Colorado Springs, Colo.

Library of Congress Cataloging-in-Publication Data
Sproul, R. C. (Robert Craig), 1965-
   Believing God : twelve biblical promises Christians struggle to accept / R. C. Sproul Jr.
      p. cm.
   Includes index.
   ISBN 978-1-56769-112-2
   1. Promises--Biblical teaching. I. Title.
   BS680.P68S67 2009
   231.7--dc22
                        2008040182

TO MY MOM AND MY DAD,
who, in His grace, believe God,
and in their grace, believe in me.

CONTENTS

FOREWORD – *Ray Comfort* ix

PREFACE xiii

ACKNOWLEDGMENTS xvii

1. ALL SCRIPTURE IS PROFITABLE (2 Timothy 3:16) 1

2. OUR HEAVENLY FATHER LOVES US (1 John 3:1). 11

3. CONFESSION, FORGIVENESS, AND CLEANSING (1 John 1: 9) 21

4. WISDOM FOR THE ASKING (James 1:5). 31

5. CHILDREN ARE A HERITAGE (Psalm 127) 41

6. THE DESIRES OF YOUR HEART (Psalm 37:4) 53

7. OPEN WINDOWS OF HEAVEN (Malachi 3:10) 65

8. MOUNTAINS CAST INTO THE SEA (Mark 11:22–24) 77

9. ALL THINGS WORK TOGETHER (Romans 8:28) 89

10. HE HAS OVERCOME THE WORLD (John 16:33) 101

11. THE GOOD WORK SHALL BE COMPLETED (Philippians 1:6). . . . 113

12. WE SHALL BE LIKE HIM (1 John 3:2) 125

SCRIPTURE INDEX. 137

THE SHADOW OF DEATH

BY RAY COMFORT

An atheist is someone who pretends that there is no God. Creation screams of the genius of the creative hand of the Almighty, yet the skeptic shuts down his mind. You can lead an atheist to evidence, but you can't make him think. He wrongly assumes that the Christian has made a decision to believe in an invisible God for whom there is no evidence. Yet all sane people "believe" in God (see Rom. 1:18–20). Creation and conscience leave the doubter without excuse. However, the requirement for salvation isn't an intellectual acknowledgement of God's existence. Rather, it entails *believing God*. Trusting Him is to implicitly trust His Word, not only accepting it as absolute truth, but appropriating it as though your very life depends on it. And it does. He who believes God repents and trusts in Him who saves us from the wrath that is to come.

An atheist once sent me an email with which I was in total agreement. He said:

> You are really convinced that you've got all the answers. You've really got yourself tricked into believing that you're 100 percent right. Well, let me tell you just one thing. Do you consider yourself to be compassionate of other humans? If you're right, as you say you are, and you believe that, then how can you sleep at night? When you speak with me, you are speaking with someone who you believe is walking directly into eternal damnation, into an endless onslaught of horrendous pain that your "loving" god created, yet you stand by and do nothing. If you believed one bit that thousands every day were falling into an eternal and unchangeable fate, you should be running the streets mad with rage at their blindness. That's equivalent to standing on a street corner and watching every person that passes you walk blindly directly into the path of a bus and die, yet you stand idly by and do nothing. You're just twiddling your thumbs, happy in the knowledge that one day that "walk" signal will shine your way across the road. Think about it. Imagine the horrors hell must have in store if the Bible is true. You're just going to allow that to happen and not care about saving anyone but yourself? If you're right, then you're an uncaring, unemotional, and purely selfish (expletive) that has no right to talk about subjects such as love and caring.

I wrote back and said that I couldn't sleep at night because I was so horrified by the thought that anyone would go to hell. Since 1982, I have risen from bed around midnight most nights each week to cry out to God to save them. I told him that for more than thirty years I have been "running" the streets, pleading with the unsaved to turn from sin. When we read the book of Acts, we see that this is nothing special. It is our reasonable service and should be the testimony of every believer who professes to possess the love of God. Charles Spurgeon knew what it was to have a deep concern for the lost. He pleaded: "Save some, O Christians! By all means, save some. From yonder flames and outer darkness, and the weeping, wailing, and gnashing of teeth, seek to save some! Let this, as in the case of the apostle, be your great, ruling object in life, that by all means you might save some."

I like R.C. Sproul Jr. I count him a friend. He truly loves God and he loves the lost. It is my earnest prayer that *Believing God* will cause you not only to trust and love your God with a greater passion, but that it will cause you also to reach out to those who sit in the shadow of death, who, apart from Jesus Christ, will face the wrath that is to come.

—Ray Comfort
Bellflower, California
August 2008

PREFACE

A ll of us tend to take offense rather easily, and I am no exception. Still, as I look back on one such occasion, I'm embarrassed that I was so offended.

Some people were involved in a discussion of my book *Almighty Over All*. In that book, I argued that, as the title suggests, God's sovereignty is over all things. Chapter after chapter looked at different situations, asking whether God was sovereign even there. Was He, I began, sovereign over creation? Was He sovereign over the fall? Was He, I eventually asked, sovereign over suffering? One particular gentleman objected to my perspective and committed the informal logical fallacy known as Bulverism. With this fallacy, rather than refuting an argument, we suggest that our opponent holds to the argument only because of some special unrelated advantage it brings. He argued that the only reason I believed in the sovereignty of God over suffering was that I had led a terribly comfortable life and had never really experienced any serious suffering.

I took deep offense. I set fingers to keyboard and presented my life as practically Job-like. I told him about the many hardships of my life, pouring on the pathos. I stepped back from my computer confident that I had made my case—my life isn't easy.

It was a foolish thing to take offense at, and my response was equally foolish. Despite that, I begin this study in believing the gracious promises of God by putting forth my suffering bona fides, or my bonafide sufferings.

My father suffers from a dilemma. The book of his with which he is most often identified is titled *The Holiness of God*. It is a potent exposition of that most potent reality. The problem is that people have so come to identify him with the holiness of God that they make the mistake of thinking he is a peculiarly holy man. He explains wisely and humbly that he was driven to study and to teach on the holiness of God not because of his holiness, but because of his lack of it. He sought to look deeply into God's holiness because of his emptiness rather than his fullness.

In like manner, I would be loathe to learn that anyone reading this book would walk away thinking of the author, "Now, there is a man who obviously believes God." The truth of the matter is that I am a man who knows that I need to believe God and that I fail bitterly. But I came to this study knowing that sin began in the garden with a failure to believe the promises of God and with the conviction that the fear of the Lord, the beginning of wisdom, begins with saying "Amen" to all that He speaks—including when He speaks blessing on us.

I knew I needed to learn better to believe God, not because my life was moving from comfort to ease, but because God—for His own good purposes, and for my good as well—was putting me through a time of significant challenge. In other words, I do not find it easy to believe God's promises because He's given me an easy life. Instead, I know I need to believe God's promises because He has, wisely, sent me some hard providences.

Five years ago, I was watching the church I had planted, Saint Peter Presbyterian, experience rapid and significant growth. Our body life, our sacred community, was enjoying such rich blessing, such sweet fellowship, that families from across the country were packing up and moving to be a part of it. My little ministry, the Highlands Study Center, was just beginning to grow. My book on homeschooling was taking off. I was getting ready to travel to South Korea to teach homeschoolers there, as well as teach at a seminary for a week or so. Three times I had been invited to teach for two weeks on a Christian radio program that ran on nearly three hundred stations. God had blessed my wife and me with six lovely children. It was a joyful time.

Then, on New Year's Eve, we received word that my dear wife had breast cancer. The next day, I lost a job that I loved, that I had prayed I would have until the day I died. My trip was cancelled.

Our church body responded in power, offering love and assistance such that we felt most potently the love of Jesus. Denise was positively heroic, never complaining through the surgeries, the chemotherapy, and the radiation. The children likewise were heroes, taking this challenge in stride and trusting in the providence of God. We determined, even while Denise was going through treatments, to move forward with our plans to build a new house. We sold our house and moved out, but our new house would not be ready for two more months. Over those months, we "moved" our rather large family twenty-four times, from this family to that, from these friends to those.

Denise's body began to heal. Her hair grew back, and we happily moved into our new home. It was not long, however, before we faced more challenges. Less than two years after Denise's treatments ended, I was diagnosed with cancer. I had surgery and went through six months of intense chemotherapy. About this same time, controversy erupted in the church where I serve, controversy fueled by a deadly combination of my sins and failures and the sins and failures of others. God had sent me a long string of hard providences.

This was the context in which I was writing this book. Throughout these ordeals, God was tender toward me. I went to bed each night not thinking about this ministry success or that, but remembering that while my enemies were rejoicing over my sin, my Father in heaven was rejoicing over my forgiveness. I went to bed knowing that even if all the world believed me to be the Devil, the Devil himself knew that I belonged to Jesus. I went to bed knowing that given how much this all hurt, it must be good for me.

God, of course, did not leave me with only words. He reminded me throughout all this that I still had friends. I woke up each morning knowing that my wife loved me and was with me. I sat down to every meal knowing that God had blessed me with flourishing olive plants (Ps. 128). Indeed, in the midst of these trials, God blessed our family with our youngest blessing, Reilly, who came to us via adoption.

Neither has God left me in such hardship. The church where I serve is prospering. God blessed the Highlands Study Center with faithful co-laborers in Dante Tremayne and Eric Owens. Denise and I are both cancer-free, and at least she again has a full head of hair. We have been busy ministering to the saints of Saint Peter and to whomever God should allow in the broader evangelical world. And I have been busy, among other things, putting this book together.

When the legions of the Serpent attack, the best way to fight back is to enter into God's good gifts, to feast at that table that He prepares in the presence of our enemies (Ps. 23). His gifts, His promises, are legion. Believing them is no fool's errand, but is to enter into wisdom's paradise. My prayer is that this little book will help urge you along that way, that it will help you step closer to the Celestial City. There we will see Him as He is and will be like Him.

—*R. C. Sproul Jr.*
Mendota, Virginia
July 2008

ACKNOWLEDGMENTS

Books are not written in vacuums. Neither are they written by loners. This book was born of a particular context and is the fruit of the labors of many.

I would like first to thank the saints of Saint Peter Presbyterian Church, where I serve. These men and women, and their beautiful children, embody what it means to believe God. Whether fasting or feasting, they move through their days with a quiet confidence in His goodness. Because He loves them, they show forth His beauty, making it all too easy for me to love them.

I would like to thank, in turn, all those who have worked with me at the Highlands Study Center over the years, including our board of directors and our faithful ministry partners. Laurence, Jonathan, Randy, Jim Bob, Eric, Dante— over the years, you have been an encouragement and an example to me.

Thanks are due as well to my friends at Reformation Trust, especially Greg Bailey. Greg was patient with me when we worked together on *Tabletalk* magazine, and has grown only more patient over the years.

Thanks, finally, again to my own dear family. You are the most present and potent witness to the grace of God in my life. In you, I remember His love.

To once more borrow an idiom from a friend, the soundtrack of this book was provided by the Tallis Scholars, Jamie Soles, and Nathan Clark George.

—*R. C. Sproul Jr.*
Mendota, Virginia
Reformation Day, 2008

CHAPTER ONE

ALL SCRIPTURE IS PROFITABLE

2 TIMOTHY 3:16

W here did it all go wrong? It is a rather important part of my particular calling as the founder of and teacher at the Highlands Study Center to decry the folly of the world. The study center exists "to help Christians live more simple, separate, and deliberate lives to the glory of God and for the building of His kingdom." That is a rather sophisticated, if not worldly, way of saying we try to help Christians be less worldly in their thinking and in their doing. But to help Christians in this way, I must be able to show the problem, to expose as foolishness the foolishness of the world, and then I must expose how even we in the church succumb to the same foolishness. Not coincidentally, people sometimes end up in despair. They come to the study center relatively content with the world, only to have the world taken away from them. That is why it is so natural for them to ask, with longing in their hearts, "Where did it all go wrong?"

It is true enough that we in the West yet enjoy the bitter remains of a once-Christian civilization. But that simply means things are not now as good as they once were. In the valley of despair, we want to know exactly when we had hit the peak and what brought on the descent. For too many of us, our historical eyes are so myopic we see only in terms of decades. We confuse civil religion with the Christian faith, and so long for the halcyon days of the 1950s. In this scenario, it was Timothy Leary or Abbie Hoffman who brought on our slide. Others look for grander giants, speculating that all was well before Darwin, Marx, or Rousseau came along. Still others aren't content with big names, but look for whole movements. No, it was the Enlightenment that started it all, or the coming of the romantics, or the rise of neoplatonism. The kingdom of God has never lacked enemies.

Sometimes when people ask my view on the matter, when they want me to pinpoint the turning point of history, I point them to Genesis 3:6b: "she took of its fruit and ate, and she also gave some to her husband who was with her, and he ate." Where did it all go wrong? In the garden of Eden.

Of course, it was not long before history took another tack. In Genesis 3:15, God promised that the Seed of the woman would crush the head of the seed of the Serpent. History, strange as it may seem from our peculiar perspective, is actually getting better and better. We miss it because we are so parochial, with respect both to space and time.

With respect to space, we judge the progress of Christ bringing all things unto submission by the standards of these United States. While this country may be the world's only superpower, it is not the entire planet. The gospel of Jesus Christ is making great strides below the equator and in the East. But since such doesn't show up on the evening news, we miss it.

In the same manner, as noted above, we look at the progress of the kingdom of God in terms of decades rather than centuries. While things may not be as good here as they were fifty years ago, we would be wise to remember that four hundred years ago you could count the number of those on this continent who were, by God's grace, among the flock of God on your fingers and toes. The conquest of all things by Jesus is not a straight, ascending line. Rather it is like a stock ticker that has both ups and downs, and yet has an upward trend.

WHAT IS CULTURAL DECLINE?

Our original question, then, ought to be modified. We know when it all went wrong and we know that Jesus is about the business of making it all right again. The narrower question is, when did our current downturn begin? To answer it well, however, we first must measure what cultural decline actually is. It is not, in the end, the embracing of Darwinian evolution. Neither is it succumbing to postmodern ideologies. As ghastly as it is, it isn't even precisely the spirit of Roe. v. Wade. Cultural decline isn't revealed ultimately in some index of leading cultural indicators. Rather, a cultural decline, like an individual's decline, is measured by one standard only, that of believing the Word of God.

The problem in the garden, after all, wasn't in the fruit. Both Adam and Eve fell simply because they didn't believe God. All that we, in turn, strive for as those in Christ is to believe God. This is what faith is, what trust is, what sanctification is. To disbelieve God is death, for a person, a family, a church, or a culture. Conversely, to believe God is life itself. We do not, after all, live by bread alone, but by every word that proceeds from the mouth of God. That is why I am writing this book.

We rightly worry that God's warnings sometimes fall on deaf ears. He tells us that judgment is coming, and it comes, precisely because we do not believe Him (remember that He promised to judge Nineveh, but because they heard Jonah and repented, He showed them grace). But as strange as it is that we don't believe His warnings, even inside the church, stranger still is that we don't believe His promises. Therefore, we are going to look, in due time, at twelve promises that God has given us in His Word, promises that Christians find difficult to believe. My goal is that as you read this book, you not only will believe each of these twelve promises, but that you will in turn believe *all* that God has promised.

This is how Paul begins chapter 3 of 2 Timothy: "But understand this, that in the last days there will come times of difficulty. For people will be lovers of self, lovers of money, proud, arrogant, abusive, disobedient to their parents, ungrateful, unholy, heartless, unappeasable, slanderous, without self-control, brutal, not loving good, treacherous, reckless, swollen with conceit, lovers of pleasure rather than lovers of God" (vv. 1–4). That sounds like us, doesn't it?

It is because we are so worldly, however, so proud, such despisers of good, that we misunderstand the nature of the problem. As children of the Enlightenment, we, both within and without the church, believe that the solution to our problem is education. It is, we think, because we are ignorant that we have become so wicked. But we must believe God enough to know that life comes from believing God and death from not believing Him. Our problem isn't that wisdom and obedience are too complicated. Our problem is that we are too sinful. The great Western sacrament is education. But look again at the list of sins Paul gives us. Will any of these be remedied by earning a higher degree? Will any of this evil dissipate if only we read the right book, attend the right seminar, or go through the right program at our local church?

Our problem isn't that we haven't sufficiently mastered the progression of sundry worldviews throughout history, though of course there is nothing wrong with that. Our problem is abundantly simple, and it is the same problem we have had from the garden—we don't believe God.

Paul proves the point in his counsel to his beloved Timothy: "You, however, have followed my teaching, my conduct, my aim in life, my faith, my patience, my love, my steadfastness, my persecutions and sufferings that happened to me at Antioch, at Iconium, and at Lystra—which persecutions I endured; yet from them all the Lord rescued me. Indeed, all who desire to live a godly life in Christ Jesus will be persecuted, while evil people and imposters will go on from bad to worse, deceiving and being deceived" (2 Tim. 3:10–13). Again, we are given a dark picture here, but one ensured to be accurate because this comes from the Holy Spirit. What must we do in evil times? "But as for you, continue in what you have learned and have firmly believed, knowing from whom you learned it and how from childhood you have been acquainted with the sacred writings, which are able to make you wise for salvation through faith in Christ Jesus" (14–15).

Paul not only tells Timothy where to go for what he needs, he tells him what he needs. This is the same Paul who, in writing to the Ephesians, warns them lest they be tossed to and fro by every wind of doctrine. That's where we are in the evangelical church. We think that we need to do what Jesus did, keeping our promises and praying that our territory would be enlarged so that we can have wild hearts filled with purpose, lest we be left behind. But God says we need to become wise through salvation through faith in Christ Jesus. And we get that by knowing the Holy Scriptures, by believing all that God has told us.

HELPING GOD'S PEOPLE TO STAND

When we think back on the grace of God in the Reformation, we too often miss where the real glory was. It was good and right and proper that Martin Luther boldly and bravely upheld the doctrines of *sola Scriptura* and *sola fide*, Scripture alone and faith alone. What was recovered can scarcely be overvalued. But we spend less time remembering Luther's quieter work. His bold stance at Worms—declaring before the tribunal that demanded he recant his biblical doctrines, "Here I stand, I can do no other, so help me God"—found flesh when he quietly, indeed secretly, set about the work of allowing all of God's people to stand. Luther left that meeting and, as soon as he stepped out of the building, a horseman swooped down and snatched up the monk. Off they rode to an unknown castle, where Luther donned the disguise of Sir George the Knight. While in hiding, he translated the Bible into the German tongue, giving God's words to God's people.

The Reformation recovered the doctrine of the perspicuity of Scripture. Though it is identified by a rather unclear term, this doctrine affirms that the Bible *is* clear. It concedes that some parts are clearer than others, but denies the notion that only the specially trained should handle such lofty prose. Such doesn't in any way deny the biblical truth that God has gifted the church with teachers (Eph. 4:11). It denies that only a teacher can grasp the teaching of the Bible.

Our problem in the evangelical church isn't, I believe, that we aren't trained well enough to grasp the hard teachings of the Bible, but that we are too worldly to believe the plain promises of the Bible. The difficulty isn't that the Bible is esoteric, but that it is profligate. The problem isn't that God speaks with a forked tongue, but that He speaks such incredible promises that we find them to be less than credible. The answer isn't to run from what God speaks, but to run to it. Thus, Paul makes perspicuous what he hopes for Timothy, and for us: "All Scripture is breathed out by God and profitable for teaching, for reproof, for correction, and for training in righteousness, that the man of God may be competent, equipped for every good work" (2 Tim. 3:16).

What are we seeking? That we might be "competent," or complete, thoroughly equipped for every good work. And that is exactly what God promises here. I know that this promise hasn't been hidden from the evangelical church. We are more than familiar with this passage. The trouble is that we don't believe it.

In my tradition, I am a part of a historical, conservative, Reformed, and Presbyterian church. We grasp at something true and important here, but we settle for far too little. That is, we see this verse as a proof-text for the inerrancy of Scripture. This passage truthfully teaches that every passage in the

Bible teaches truthfully all that it teaches. But if we would believe God, we not only must believe this verse is without error, we also must believe, because we believe that this verse is without error, that all the Bible is without error.

The problem is that this probably isn't the exact point that Paul had in mind here. Paul wasn't writing Timothy to warn him that men who would deny that the Bible is without error would come into the church millennia later. Rather, he wanted Timothy to know that because the Bible is breathed out by God, it is not only true, but profitable for doctrine.

Here again, we delightedly concur. The Bible *is* profitable for doctrine. But once again, at least in the circles I run in, we too often stop there. My theological tradition is known for being persnickety about its theology. That's a good thing. If we're going to be sloppy, the last place we want to be that way is in dealing with our understanding of the things of God. But doctrine not only isn't the whole of the Christian life, it isn't the whole focus of this passage. The Bible here promises that the Bible is profitable for reproof, correction, and instruction in righteousness.

Again, my theological tradition tends to wiggle out from the implications here. Because we are, again, wisely careful with our doctrine, we make the mistake of thinking that Paul is stuttering here. We believe in reproof, as long as what we are being reproved for is wrong doctrine. We believe in correction, as long as we are having our doctrine corrected. Paul, however, is leading us somewhere. What we need is instruction in righteousness, which is rather a different standard of spiritual maturity than having our theological i's dotted and t's crossed. That means, in turn, that we do not believe this promise, because we have missed its point.

ALL OF THE BIBLE FOR ALL TIMES

We miss both the nature and the scope of the promise. We are told that not simply our favorite parts of the Bible, the red letters in our Bibles, or the epistles of Paul are good for instruction in righteousness, but *all* the Bible. Wherever we go in the Word of God, there we find power for changing our lives. We cannot write parts of it off by "contextualizing" it, whereby, while claiming to believe the Bible is God's Word, we treat some of it as no longer applicable to us. We do this by constructing elaborate interpretive systems that affirm that parts of the Bible were for then, parts are for now, and still more parts are for later.

A friend once asked my counsel about a touchy ethical issue. He was eager to apply God's Word to his situation, so he asked me, "Does the Bible anywhere address this particular issue?"

"Yes," I told him, "I believe in Deuteronomy, we are told this about that particular issue."

Unfortunately, he wasn't satisfied. This "Bible-believing" Christian asked then, "Is there anything in the New Testament that talks about this?"

I hesitated a moment and then told him, "Yes, Jesus said in the Sermon on the Mount"—and you could see the relief in his eyes—"not an iota, not a dot, will pass from the Law until all is accomplished" (Matt. 5:18b). It is all the Bible, even the parts that make us uncomfortable (perhaps especially the parts that make us uncomfortable), that corrects, reproves, and instructs us in righteousness.

There are, however, still more subtle ways in which we fail to believe this promise. I'm afraid that we think the Bible is magic in a somewhat superstitious way. Too often we think that when we sit down and open the Bible that the Devil scurries away like a vampire confronted by garlic. The truth of the matter is that the Devil sits down right beside us. He encourages us in the diabolical art of what I call "simultaneous translation." Just as at the United Nations gifted linguists hear the words of the speaker and in an instant repeat those words in another language, so we, as our eyes roll across the page, translate what we are reading. There we are, sitting down at our quiet time. We come across this familiar passage, one that we may have even committed to memory. Our eyes see, "All Scripture is breathed out by God and profitable for teaching, for reproof, for correction, and for training in righteousness, that the man of God may be competent, equipped for every good work," and we say to ourselves in the quiet of our minds, "The Bible is good." Of course the Bible is good, but our translation of it, or rather our reduction of it, has stripped it of its power.

I suspect we do this because we are fundamentally indifferent about our calling. If I were to promise you that I would eat ten watermelons in one sitting, you might have trouble believing me. More important, however, you probably wouldn't much care whether I could do it. Simply put, we need to develop a biblical hunger for the thing promised. We are told here that we can be made complete, thoroughly equipped for every good work. If you're like me, you probably spend far more time daydreaming about what it might be like to win the lottery than you do wondering what it might be like if you took enormous strides in your sanctification, if you became a hero of the faith, if you better reflected the glory of Jesus in all that you do. If we spent more time entering into the kind of anguish the apostle Paul goes through in Romans 7—"I do not do the good I want, but the evil I do not want is what I keep on doing. . . . Wretched man that I am! Who will deliver me from this body of death?" (vv. 19, 24)—then perhaps we would rejoice when confronted with this sure promise from God. All Scripture is able to make us complete, thoroughly equipped for every good work.

Our problem, however, may follow a different tack. Perhaps we have a profound hunger and thirst for righteousness. Maybe our hearts long to grow in grace. Maybe, however, we need to start with this very passage. It could be that our hunger is thwarted by our very unbelief. We come to this promise and are embarrassed by it. It is too much, too grand, too good to be true. It is a good thing that those words of wisdom, "If something seems too good to be true, it probably is," carry that important hedge, "probably." When God makes a promise, unlike every other promise that we encounter, it is too good *not* to be true. God not only has given us the promise in His Word, He has given us the promise of His Word. We are equipped, ready to go. We do not need the latest Christian fad to come down the pike. We need instead the oldest Christian habit to come down the pike. We need to read, to understand, and most important, to believe the Word of God.

This is God's promise, that if we will avail ourselves of the Word of God, we will find it profitable for doctrine. The Bible isn't a wax nose that can be molded and shaped any way we please. No, the Bible shapes us and our doctrine. As Luther put it to Erasmus of Rotterdam, *Spiritus Sanctus non est skepticus.* "The Holy Spirit is not a skeptic." As the Spirit breathed out His Word, He equipped us for finding sound doctrine.

This is God's promise, that if we will avail ourselves of the Word of God, we will find it profitable for reproof. We are not stuck in our solipsistic errors. We can see ourselves from outside ourselves, by the power of His Word. It will reprove our errors, in our thinking, in our feeling, and in our doing; in our minds, in our hearts, and in our hands.

This is God's promise, that if we will avail ourselves of the Word of God, we will find it profitable for correction. Where we err, it will set us on the right path. Like the rod and staff of our Great Shepherd, it will comfort us, for it will keep us on the narrow way. Where we walk crooked, it will make our paths straight.

This is God's promise, that if we will avail ourselves of the Word of God, we will find it profitable for instruction in righteousness. It will bring us closer to our end, when we will be like Him, for we shall see Him as He is. We will become ever more complete, thoroughly equipped for every good work. If we would lay hold of these promises, we must look to His Word, that we might in turn believe His Word.

CHAPTER TWO

OUR HEAVENLY
FATHER LOVES US

1 JOHN 3:1

I have been blessed, because of my slightly peculiar upbringing, to have met some of our time's greatest theologians. My father's work brought him, and through him me, into contact with some of the ablest thinkers and communicators that God has given us. I was in high school when I began to appreciate this. I met bestselling authors and teachers on the most-listened-to radio programs. But of all the giants I met, one stood above all the others. It is no coincidence that my greatest theological hero had the same theological hero I had. I learned to love and respect Dr. John Gerstner both because my father so loved him and because of why he loved him.

Though Dr. Gerstner wasn't as well known as some of the others I met, he had two gifts out of all due proportion. First, he had a mind so logical that Sherlock Holmes could not have kept up. Like a master chess player, in the context of a theological argument, Dr. Gerstner not only knew what your next four arguments would be, he understood the necessary implications of every one of them, plus the implications of the arguments you wouldn't make.

But what so shocked those who had merely read Dr. Gerstner or heard him teach was to be confronted with the one quality that exceeded the precision of his mind, and that was the humility of his heart. These gifts, however, do tie together. It was because Dr. Gerstner was convinced of the gospel truth that God is sovereign over all things that he was convinced that he had nothing that had not been given to him. He was right, of course, but such didn't change the fact that he had been given much.

These two qualities, his humility and his towering intellect, collided once right in front of me. Dr. Gerstner was invited to speak at a conference where I was working. One of my assignments was to introduce the good doctor to the assembled crowd. For about a micro-second I was delighted. But then I saw my problem. How could I communicate the depths of my respect and admiration while at the same time not embarrassing my hero? To put it another way, I wondered how I could honor him while honoring him. I wanted to tell the crowd what a great man he was. The great man would want me to do no such thing. My solution was a little devious. If one were to describe Dr. Gerstner, the first attribute noted would be the humility. The second would be the intellect. But the third would be that he was as deaf as a stump. I introduced him the way I wanted to introduce him. I showered him with praise, trusting that he wasn't hearing a word I was saying. In other words, I did exactly the wrong thing. Humility is expressed best not with flowery odes but through rather ordinary obedience.

Obedience is better even than the flattery of imitation. We ought to come to God's law as King David did, delighting in it, meditating on it, and obeying it. Too often, however, we "honor" God by creating our own law, making ourselves more pious than Him. God says, "Don't eat," and we say, "Don't touch." God says, "Give ten percent," and we say, "Give twenty

percent." Like the Pharisees before us, we add to God's law, then expect Him
to pat us on the back. This problem of seeking a piety greater than God's,
however, gets no uglier than when we apply it to ourselves.

My father tells a story from his days as a college professor. Like most pro-
fessors, he spent several hours a week in his office meeting with students. A
young lady came to see him, deeply troubled. It seems she had been behaving
inappropriately with her boyfriend. She explained that her hardship was less
about what she had done and more about her current condition—though
she had repented frequently and with great vigor, she didn't feel forgiven for
her sin. She poured out her story and her heart to my father, who responded
with great pastoral wisdom.

"I think I know what you need to do," he said. "I'd suggest that you go
back to your dorm room, get on your knees, and plead with God to forgive
you of your sin."

The poor girl was even more heartbroken after that. "Dr. Sproul," she
said, "I'm afraid you haven't been listening. Repenting is all I've been doing,
and it hasn't done any good."

"I have heard you just fine," my father replied. "This time when you
repent, I don't want you to repent for what happened with your boyfriend. I
want to you beg God to forgive you for not believing His promises. He said,
'If we confess our sins, he is faithful and just to forgive us our sins and to
cleanse us from all unrighteousness' (1 John 1:9). God is utterly unimpressed
with our efforts to beat ourselves psychologically for our sins. What He wants
is a true humility that will manifest itself as faith, as believing God."

There are few promises of God more difficult to believe than the promise
of His forgiveness. Therefore, we will look at 1 John 1:9 in the next chapter.
But truth be told, God does more than merely forgive us. John clues us into
an even grander promise just a few chapters later: "See what kind of love the
Father has given to us, that we should be called children of God" (1 John 3:1).
We are doing God no favors if we cry out in light of this promise, "We're not

worthy." Of course we're not worthy. That's pretty much the point, isn't it? The greatness of the promise isn't that He has made us worthy to be called His children. This text isn't evidence of our glory. It is evidence of God's condescension to us. It is evidence of yet another thing we have a hard time believing in—God's love for us.

WRIGGLING AWAY FROM AN OVERWHELMING PROMISE

In fact, let's begin there. The text tells us that God loves us. We're willing to concede that God is willing to forgive us. Such is too obvious to deny. We're even willing to concede that God is gracious and kind to us. He gives us this day our daily bread. He showers us with blessings. But love us? That's too much. Oh, we'll admit it in our creeds. We'll cave to the plain teaching in our studies. What we won't do is actually believe this in our hearts. We misuse our minds to wriggle away from this overwhelming promise.

There are any number of stratagems we're willing to try. Some of us break out wisdom we've learned from various theories of counseling. Love, these theories tell us, is more of an action than an emotion. To say, then, that God loves us is really to say nothing more than that He forgives us, that He is gracious to us. In this manner, we escape the hard emotional truth that while love may be more than emotion, it is not less. Yes, God is gracious to us. But our text tells us that God loves us with real, emotive love.

Sometimes we seek to avoid the import and power of this promise by looking at God's love from a neoorthodox perspective. The neoorthodox movement prided itself on its desire to affirm and protect the doctrine of God's transcendence. God is not simply a grown-up man. He is different, other. All of this is true. But we make a grave mistake if we allow this otherness to obliterate any connection. We are still made in His image. Of course, His love isn't exactly like our love. But this doesn't diminish the promise;

rather, it amplifies it. His love, unlike ours, is pure, constant, unfailing. His love, like ours, is love.

Perhaps the soundest escape route is to affirm the obvious. God's character is such that He cannot ultimately love that which is unlovely. And we, in ourselves, are decidedly unlovely. Christ, however, is altogether lovely. Thus, what He loves in us, that we might be called His children, is Christ in us. So when the text says He loves us, it really means He loves His Son. Once again, it's all true. But what is likewise true is that we are in union with His Son. Our union with Him is not a mere legal fiction, but has a reality grounded in reality. It is so real that not only are we allowed to be called His children, but as John tells us in the very next verse, "Beloved, we *are* God's children now" (1 John 3:2a, emphasis added). God our Father really loves us because He really loves Him, and we are really in union with Him. Our calling then, for the rest of our lives, and on into eternity, is to seek to get our hearts and our minds around this staggering reality that, if we are in Christ, then the God of all the universe actually, truly, really, emotionally loves us, and loves us as His children.

Five feet away from me as I write is my youngest son. He came into our family just two weeks ago. He came to us, however, in an unusual way. He was born to parents different from my wife and me. Our son came to us through the miracle of adoption. My dear wife and I understand that there will come a time when our son will struggle with believing that we love him. He may, for a time, feel either the need to test our love or to prove himself worthy of our love. But he is our son, our beloved son.

And so we all, if we are in Christ, are so loved that we have been adopted into the very family of God. In this context, our adoption reminds us that in ourselves we are not worthy of this calling. We are not by nature little gods. We are instead by nature rebels against and haters of God, soldiers of the Serpent. But we have not only been forgiven, we have been adopted.

I'm afraid Protestants, in rightly defending the reality of the legal transaction inherent in the work of Christ, miss out on other emphases of the Bible.

It is a true joy and delight that in Christ we have been declared by the Judge of all the universe to be just. He will hold our sins against us no more. If by His grace we trust in the finished work of His Son, we have been forgiven and are at peace with Him. This is sufficient to fill us with all joy, but it is woefully lacking in showing forth the fullness of what Christ accomplished for us.

MUCH MORE THAN A LEGAL ARRANGEMENT

God's covenant of grace isn't simply a legal arrangement, any more than our marriage covenants are merely legal arrangements. Yes, there is a legal side to covenant, but we too often miss the familial side. Covenant, in fact, is the marriage of the legal and the familial. God does not merely welcome us into His kingdom because He's such a nice guy, a sweet-hearted father. By no means. Blood had to be spilled. The penalty had to be paid. But the end result wasn't merely acquittal. When you stand before the judgment seat and God asks you how you plead, if you are wise you will plead the blood of Christ. When you have done so, however, God will not merely look over His glasses at you, shuffle a few papers, bang His celestial gavel, and say: "Not guilty. Next." No, the image of what happens at the death of the saint is rather different. God will indeed be in a robe, but He, seeing you coming from afar off, will gird up the hems of His robe and run to meet you. He will throw His arms about your neck and cry out, "My son, My son." He will command that a robe and a ring be brought for you, and that the fatted calf be killed so that a feast might be held for you.

We are not merely, according to this promise, sinners found not guilty, but we are adopted sons and daughters. We are loved sons and daughters. This is why adoption is such a beautiful description. It is both legal and familial. Legally speaking, in ourselves we are not at all worthy to be His children. We are not good enough. We are by nature not His children, but children of wrath. But He has set His love on us. He has chosen us, that we should be His children.

John goes still further. Lest we take his teaching and reduce it to a metaphor, he brings us back to reality. It isn't simply that God has given a special dispensation that we can be *called* His children. It's not an honorary designation. Instead, "we are." That is, we are not merely called His children, we are His children. We are the sons of God. Here we have to be doubly careful. We do not, as God's children, take on all the qualities of God. We do not, because of our adoption, become omnipotent. We do not, when we are brought into His family, suddenly become self-existent beings with no beginning in time. The second element of our care, however, is that we must not let the first element diminish the reality. A real change takes place in our adoption, and we really are His children.

There are three things we need to grasp if we would grow in believing God here. First is what I have belabored. What a staggering shock—He loves us as His sons. Or, equally staggering, we are His sons and He loves us. How might we differ if we believed simply this? How might we cease to clamor and claw our way toward the approval of men? How might we enjoy the fruit of joy, peace, and patience because our deepest longing has been fulfilled? How might our fears dissipate if we knew deep in our hearts that we are the beloved children of the Lord of all things? How might we live in peace with the brethren if we knew not only that we are the children of God, but so are they? That not only are we beloved of the Father, but so are they? How might we put to death the sins of slander and gossip if we knew we are His children?

Second, how firm might the peace be if we understood that this real, emotive love from our Father is an unchangeable love? God is not some date from junior high. He doesn't write our name on His notebook, only to erase it when some new love comes along. If we are His children now, if He loves us now, then we can know for certain, for the rest of our lives, no matter the hardship of circumstance, that we will always be His children and that He will always love us.

I remind my children of this reflected fact when I discipline them. The process requires me to inflict pain on the children. The children always then repent to me. They hug me and say, "I'm sorry, Daddy." And Daddy always replies: "I forgive you and I love you. I not only love you, but will always love you. In fact, I loved you even in the midst of the pain." Our Father loves us with an unshakable love. Even His discipline is out of love alone. The scales of justice were evened two thousand years ago. Now He chastens precisely because of His love, precisely because we are His children.

There is one more place where the legal and the familial kiss in the outworking of covenant. We see it when the family gathers together to hear read a man's "Last Will and Testament." That word *testament* is just another word for *covenant*. What happens at such an event is legal in the sense that property is passed on, usually from one generation of a given family to the next. But it is also familial because the last words of the departed are often read to those he has left behind. Our heavenly Father, of course, will never and can never die. That doesn't change the truth, however, that we are His heirs in Christ. Third, then, we have the inheritance of sons.

AN INHERITANCE OF GLOBAL PROPORTIONS

What does our Father have to give us? Much has been made in some evangelical circles of the promise God made to Abraham as it relates to the borders of Israel. Debates over God's intentions then intersect with what we read in the daily papers now. Whatever might be sound or unsound on different sides of these arguments, both, I'm afraid, miss something rather significant later in the Bible. The rights or non-rights of Abraham's physical descendents pale in comparison to another promise that Jesus made. In the Sermon on the Mount, Jesus, among other ends, seeks to instill in us the qualities that mark the heirs of the kingdom. He says that they will be blessed if they are poor in Spirit, if they mourn, if they hunger and thirst for righteousness, if they are merciful, if they are pure in heart, if they are peacemakers, and if they are persecuted. The blessings He promises, however, are not always vague. The meek, He tells us, will inherit the earth. Who is meek? Only Jesus fits the bill for all these blessings. But in union with Him we receive all these blessings. In Him we are meek, His meek children who will inherit all the earth. What's in God's will for us? The entire planet, because the earth is the Lord's and the fullness thereof. Such is what we will inherit.

Our Father, however, doesn't merely own the cattle on a thousand hills; He owns all good things. Thus, our inheritance isn't merely the wealth of land, but the very goodness we strive toward. That is, the joy isn't simply that we'll be rich, but that we'll be good. It is because of His wealth of goodness that we shall be good. It is out of the fullness of His beauty that we shall inherit beauty. This is why eye has not seen nor ear heard, nor has it entered into the heart of man the things that God has prepared for those who love Him.

Our little minds can't get around all that He has promised His children. As His children, however, we must try. We have to meditate on this promise and learn to rejoice in its fullness. This is the fullness of joy that we have been promised. Because we believe it to be too good to be true, we demonstrate that we are not good enough to believe it, that we lack the faith to which we are called. Is this not John's point? Isn't he enjoining us to understand the depth of the love of our Father? "See what kind of love the Father has given to us. . . ." Do you want to know how much love this is? First, consider how much an earthly father would love his own child. Then remove from the equation every bit of selfishness, insecurity, and sin from the father. There you have a reflection, for this imaginary sin-free father is still but a man. The love of our Father is the love of our heavenly Father. He is not only perfect, but is infinite in all His perfections. That means that He loves us not only immutably, but infinitely. Our heavenly Father loves us with all that He is, and all that He is He is perfectly.

That brings us back once again to our inheritance. It isn't just the world He made that we will receive. It isn't just the virtues that He calls us to that we will receive. Our Father, because He can never die, makes us heirs of the one thing worth having, the very reality of which every other blessing is but a reflection. What we inherit, and what will delight us into eternity, is God Himself. He is His greatest possession, and as His heirs we will inherit Him. Of course, we will always be His. He, after all, is our Father and our Maker. But the glory of His grace is that He has also promised that He will be ours. He is our exceedingly great reward.

We live by sight. We are yet mired in our sin and surrounded by others so mired. We fret and we worry, afraid that we won't get what's coming to us, or, worse, afraid that we will get what was coming to us, that in the end we will receive justice and judgment from God rather than grace and adoption. If we are in Christ, however, we won't get what was coming to us. Jesus already took that for us. So we will get what's coming to Him. For we are joint heirs of the only begotten, the other brethren of the Firstborn. May He be pleased to work in us such that we would believe Him, and all that He has promised His children.

CHAPTER THREE

CONFESSION, FORGIVENESS, AND CLEANSING

1 JOHN 1:9

T here is a reason we have such a struggle believing that our Father loves us. That reason is simple enough—we are all Pelagians at heart.

In the late fourth century, Pelagius made a name for himself when he responded angrily to a published prayer of Saint Augustine. Augustine prayed, "O Lord, command what Thou wilt, and grant what Thou dost command." Augustine wanted to affirm God's sovereign authority first. God, as the Maker of all things, has the right to command anything He wishes. Augustine, in his prayer, affirmed that authority. He then affirmed God's sovereign power to make obedience possible. "Grant what Thou dost command" means that obedience itself is a gift from God. Pelagius thought otherwise, arguing that

God could command, morally speaking, only that which we have the ability to do. He declared that God would be unjust if He commanded us to do something we aren't able to do. Based on this reasoning, Pelagius argued that we have the capacity in ourselves to keep even God's command that we must be perfect, that we must obey the whole of His law.

Pelagius denied the doctrine of original sin. He held that Adam's sin affected Adam only, and that all men born after him have it in themselves to obey God perfectly. Pelagius' view eventually was roundly condemned as heresy by the church, but he still continues to haunt us. It is precisely because of the effects of sin in each of us that we are still foolish enough, even inside the church, to believe that we can earn God's favor. Our lips cry out that we are justified by faith alone, and that even faith is a gift from God. The trouble is, we still, in the dark corners of our hearts, tend to think we can merit God's grace. Some of us think we can do this by keeping our quiet times. Others of us think we earn His favor by our precise formulations of theological doctrines.

Of course, our careful doctrine itself reminds us that we can't earn God's favor. So we vacillate between pride and humility, between ease and despair. To put it more clearly, we reflect the folly of Pelagius when we cry out in despair, "We're not worthy," when confronted with the grace of God. But we reflect the wisdom of Augustine when we cry out with joy, "We're not worthy," when confronted with the grace of God. As Pelagians, we mourn because we know we have missed the mark, but foolishly think we missed it just barely. We think we almost earned peace with God and weep that we came up short. That means that our despair is less the result of not having God's love and more the result of having failed to reach our goal. We feel bad about ourselves because we did not win the prize.

Pelagianism was roundly condemned because it was not merely a wrong turn theologically speaking. It wasn't the logical conclusion of some small error. Instead, it was the polar opposite of biblical Christianity. The Christian faith begins with the profession that we are not worthy. We do not profess that we are *almost* worthy, that we fell just a touch short of being worthy, that we could have been worthy if only we had tried harder. No, we are not worthy, and never would come close on our own. There is nothing good in us.

WHERE SIN IS DENIED, TRUTH IS ABSENT

John the beloved disciple makes this very point in the first chapter of his first epistle. He writes, "If we say we have no sin, we deceive ourselves, and the truth is not in us" (v. 8). Now this ought to capture our attention. This is one of very few passages in the Scriptures that give us a clear, measurable standard by which to answer one compelling question: am I a Christian or not? John here lays out a surefire sign by which we might know we are outside the kingdom of God. It's not the only sign, but it is a sufficient sign. If we say we have no sin, the truth is not in us. It seems likely that John's conclusion carries double freight. First, if we say we are without sin, then we say something that is not true. We are wrong. We are in error. But John seems to suggest something far stronger. If we say we are without sin, we do not merely say something false, but the truth is not in us. We are not, it seems, indwelt by the very Spirit of truth.

That said, there are probably varying levels of this folly. One need not embrace the heterodox arguments of the perfectionists to drink of this foolishness. Even we who hold onto the doctrine of original sin and believe sin will be with us always on this side of the veil can commit this error, to a lesser degree. Those of us who are firm in our commitment to Augustinianism still find ways to diminish the scope and severity of our sins. We sometimes compare our transgressions to those of others, falling into the trap of the Pharisee who prayed: "God, I thank you that I am not like other men, extortioners, unjust, adulterers, or even like this tax collector. I fast twice a week; I give tithes of all that I get" (Luke 18:11b–12). We are experts at rationalizing our sins, explaining away our disobedience. We even twist the Word of God and call good that which God calls evil.

We are given in this parable, however, a counter-example. Jesus defines for us the very essence of saving faith, shockingly, in the person of the tax collector. His prayer is not as ornate as that of the Pharisee. It may not even be more sincere. (That is, the Pharisee may actually believe in his own goodness.) But it is more true and more powerful. The text tells us, "But the tax collector, standing far off, would not even lift up his eyes to heaven, but beat his breast, saying, 'God, be merciful to me, a sinner!'" (v. 13).

Jesus doesn't merely tell us that the first man did poorly while the second did well. These different prayers aren't given to us so that we might know a better way to pray. They are given so that we might know the very path to heaven. "I tell you," Jesus says, "this man went down to his house justified, rather than the other. For everyone who exalts himself will be humbled, but the one who humbles himself will be exalted" (v. 14). The gap between these prayers is but a reflection of the great chasm that separates heaven and hell.

Since the time of the Reformation, the Protestant church has affirmed as a fundamental conviction the doctrine of *sola fide*, faith alone. We affirm that we are justified, made right with God, not through our own righteousness, but by the righteousness of Christ, which becomes ours by faith. Some have tried to twist this message. They suggest that it is foolish to teach that one can be saved by believing in *sola fide*, in justification by faith alone. They are as right as rain. Such would indeed be a foolish thing to teach. But no one says we are saved by believing in faith alone. Instead, we say that it is faith alone that brings us the work of Christ, which in turn saves us. To put it another way, no one will enter the kingdom if, standing before the judgment seat of God, they cry out, "I believe in justification by faith alone." No. But no one will be found just there unless they trust in the finished work of Christ alone. It isn't a proper formulation of doctrine that gets anyone in. What gets us in is "God, be merciful to me, a sinner!"

This great truth, however, not only gets us into the kingdom of God, it keeps us there. Our Pelagianism creeps back up on us when we confess that we were, at the moment of our conversion, made right with God and forgiven of all our past sins, but the future is still up in the air. Prior to conversion, we're willing to accept our need for Christ, but now, shouldn't we, with the indwelling of the Holy Spirit, be able to keep and obey God's law? Even if we aren't convinced that after conversion we ought to be able to keep the law, we do tend to diminish the reality of the sin that remains in our lives.

FINDING ASSURANCE AMID SIN

In my years as a pastor, the most frequent question I have received is, "How can I know if I am saved?" The question isn't an apologetical one, such as, "How can I know that the Bible is true?" It isn't a theological one, like, "How can I know that the Bible teaches I must trust in Christ alone for my salvation?" Instead, it is an assurance question: "How can I know that I truly believe the gospel?" What typically prompts the uncertainty is an all-too-real certainty about the remaining sin in the person's life. What are we left to do in such circumstances? We could take a mathematically precise measurement of sin in our lives, which likely would cause us to despair all the more. Or we could gaze more deeply into our navels, trying to find inwardly an outward measure of faith. (And here we find another Pelagian temptation, thinking that the depth of our doubt and sorrow somehow will earn God's favor.)

The answer to every question, every hardship, however, is this: repent and believe the gospel. The question ought not to be, "Was I saved yesterday; did I believe yesterday?" What difference could that possibly make? My reply to the soul doubting his salvation is simple enough: "Do you trust in the finished work of Christ alone? Do you repent and believe?" I ask these questions because of the promise that God has made: "If we confess our sins, he is faithful and just to forgive us our sins and to cleanse us from all unrighteous-ness" (1 John 1:9).

One need not be an adult to struggle to believe this promise. In our family of seven children, we have a great deal of routine. We have schedules that we keep, patterns that we follow to keep our household from descending into chaos. Those habits extend even to the ways in which we discipline our children. We have a liturgy that we follow there, a liturgy that begins with judgment but ends with gospel. Suppose my oldest son has decided to play Picasso with his peanut butter sandwich. Suppose he has smeared peanut butter all over the kitchen wall. He has never done such a thing, mind you, but he has, from time to time, sinned. Our pattern is this. First, I take my son to someplace private. I ask him, "Did you smear your peanut butter sandwich on the wall?"

"Yes, Daddy" he replies.

"Are you allowed to do this?"

"No, Daddy."

At this point, I administer a brief but painful corrective to my son, at which point he hugs me and I hug him back. Then he tells me, "I'm sorry, Daddy," and I tell him, "Daddy forgives you, son, and Daddy loves you, all the time."

Next my son says this three-part prayer: "Dear Lord, please forgive me for disobeying and smearing my peanut butter sandwich on the wall. Thank you that Jesus died for my sins so that I can be forgiven. Please help me to be more obedient."

By this point, my son's tears have usually dried up. But if they haven't yet, if he is struggling to accept my forgiveness, I look my son in the eye and ask him this: "Son, what has God promised us?"

He replies, "If we confess our sins, he is faithful and just to forgive us our sins and to cleanse us from all unrighteousness." In all likelihood, at this point I have tears in my eyes as I embrace my son once more and we rejoice in the glory of the gospel.

Understand that when I punish my children, I do so not to even the scales of justice. My action isn't retributive. The just punishment due to my children (and to my wife and me for that matter) was given two thousand years ago on Calvary. All my children's sins, past, present, and future, are forgiven. But we are still called to repent.

Here we walk a thin line. We do not want to view our verbal confession as magic words that lose their power over time. That is, heaven is not populated merely by those who managed to squeeze in a confession just before they died, with no time for another sin to slip through. On the other hand, we cannot adopt a cavalier attitude: "Hey, I confessed when I walked down the aisle. Why do I need to confess again?" As is so often the case, the answer is balance. Our sins are forgiven, now and forever, if we are in Christ. But we remember the very joy of our salvation each time we confess our sins.

A GOD BOTH FAITHFUL AND JUST

This is God's promise. There are two parts to it. First, if we confess our sins, He is "faithful and just" to forgive us our sins. Herein is the real danger. When we fail to believe His promises, we fail to believe that He is faithful. We think that His promises are much like ours, idle words designed to get what we want. But our Father is not like us. He has promised. And He alone cannot break His promise. It is His fidelity, not our worthiness, that guarantees the forgiveness. We slip once again into the folly of Pelagianism when we think that He forgives us because we are worthy, and so when we slip below some standard of worthiness, we think He won't forgive us. We are sinners, but He is faithful, and it is by His faithfulness that He forgives.

In what ways is God *faithful* in forgiveness? First, He is faithful to His promises, that if we call on the name of His Son we will be saved. This is His offer to us, free and certain. He is faithful to His Word. Second, He is faithful to the promises He made to our parents. He told them, if they were His, that He would in turn be God to their children. Third, and most important of all, He is faithful to His Son. He keeps His promise to Him. It was for the promised bride that Christ went through His humiliation. The Father keeps His promise to His Son, and through Him, to all those who are adopted into His family.

God not only is faithful to forgive us, however, but *just* to do so. Sometimes I'm afraid we are so eager to praise God for His mercy to us that we misunderstand it, and in a backward sort of way, denigrate it. That is, too often we make the mistake of thinking that we are forgiven for our sins just because God decided to be nice and to look the other way, that He winked at our sins. God is indeed merciful. And He does not remember our sins. They are as far from us as the east is from the west. But it is just that such should be so. Our debt is no more not because He whom we owe forgave it, but because it was paid. He is just to forgive us because He poured out the just punishment for our sins on His Son. And He is just to vindicate us. He raised His Son from the dead to demonstrate that He did not die for His sins, but for ours. In union with Him, raised with Him, we too are vindicated. The Judge of all the earth does judge rightly when He says that sinners like us are not guilty. Jesus paid our debt, and we owe no more. In fact, it would be unjust for God to demand retribution for sins covered on Calvary. In short, it is just that He should forgive us our sins, not because we are worthy, but because worthy is the Lamb.

When we stop with the promise of forgiveness, as grand and as shocking as it is, we still miss out on the fullness of the promise. For we long not merely to have God's judgment pass over us, but to be made white as snow. The promise of the gospel isn't just that we won't be judged, but that, in the end, we will be good. Thus, John tells us that not only does He forgive us for our sins, He cleanses us from all unrighteousness. Now that's a grand promise.

Indeed, one of the greatest mysteries for me about the afterlife is found right here. How, I wonder, can I continue to be me, to have a consciousness that is connected to and continues from what I have now, that will have no sin? I wouldn't recognize me, and I doubt anyone else would either. I'm afraid I'm so puzzled by this because I don't spend enough time thinking about this promise and the promise of my sanctification. I'm afraid that in my tradition, we think of sanctification as a process at best and as a doctrine at worst. But we almost never see it as John shows it to us here, as a promise.

This is His promise. As we despair in our sin, not only are we promised forgiveness, we are promised cleansing. The sorrow that follows in the wake of our sins is crushed now by gospel forgiveness. It is also crushed then, that is, in the future, by gospel cleansing. We need to believe His promises and crush the despair.

In short, we need to look at our sanctification the way God told Joshua to look at the Promised Land. Joshua, after forty years of wandering in the wilderness, is about to take his ragtag army of nomads into Palestine, a land flowing with milk and honey, but one inhabited by great and mighty men. He is called to fight a war that, from a human perspective, he has no chance of winning. His army consists of the children of the cowards who feared to cross the Jordan forty years earlier. Moses, the great prophet, has gone on to his reward. Would you not, were you in Joshua's sandals, fear? Would you not ask God to give you a glimpse into the future, a sign of promise?

God gives instructions. He gives orders. But He gives no sign. As the Israelites approach the great walled city of Jericho, the text tells us, "Now Jericho was shut up inside and outside because of the people of Israel. None went out, and none came in" (Josh. 6:1). The battle has not yet taken place. God's enemies are hiding in their seemingly impregnable fortress. But hear what God says to Joshua: "And the LORD said to Joshua, 'See, I have given Jericho into your hand, with its king and mighty men of valor'" (v. 2). God creates here a new tense in any language, a grammatical structure I call "God's prophetic present." That king and those soldiers, if they aren't comfortable in their homes, are armed to the teeth and waiting. God doesn't say, "Don't worry, I promise I will give you this city." He says instead that He has *already* given Joshua the city. This is God's power. His promise is so certain that it is past before it is fulfilled.

This is true, however, of all of God's promises. His Word is to reality what Midas' touch was to gold. He speaks and it is so. If God promises that the sun will not come up tomorrow, it is as certain as the fact that it came up today. And if God promises to forgive us our sins, they are forgiven. It is finished. If He promises to cleanse us from all unrighteousness, then it is done, certain. Our proper response to the despair of present sin is to believe the future promises of God. This we know with as much certainty as, if not more than, Joshua experienced *after* the battle of Jericho—that we are forgiven, and nothing will keep us from utter perfection. See, He has so promised.

CHAPTER FOUR

WISDOM FOR THE ASKING

JAMES 1:5

I suspect I'm like a lot of people in that I tend to think most people are pretty much like me. I tend to think others not only think like me, but tend to sin like me. Thus, my concerns about the habits of the church at large tend to follow my concerns about my weaknesses and failures. I preach against my own sin, believing that it is not all that unusual. There is wisdom here, but danger as well. When we are our own yardsticks, it is rather easy to miss how crooked we are. In order to get a real handle on what God's Word says, we need to step outside what is merely normal to us and seek to see the Bible objectively, to use it as a mirror.

Too often it is the "normal" that encourages us to practice simultaneous translation. We come to the Bible expecting little, so we miss the greatness of the promises. We reduce them down to something manageable, something safe. Sometimes the Bible is so straightforward in what it promises, however, that we can't turn it into something safe. What we do instead is determine that while we can't know what the text means, it certainly can't mean what it says. Once more, I suspect that many Christians do this, because I know that I do this.

I'm confident I'm not alone among Christians when it comes to certain other things as well. First, I have had for decades now a deep longing for wisdom. Second, like that old country song about looking for love, I have spent most of my life looking for wisdom in precisely the wrong places. Because I was enamored with the wisdom of this world, for too long I believed that that would be where I would find wisdom.

I remember spending hours as a teenager scanning the books in my father's library. Mercy, he had nearly a dozen Bibles. He not only had God's Word, but a fair representation of the work of those teachers with which God has blessed the church from the beginning. There were the complete works of Martin Luther and the collected writings of Jonathan Edwards. My father had, and still has, as do I now, a complete set of John Calvin's commentaries on the Bible.

Instead of reading these wise works, however, I chose books from an obscure corner of his library. I found the books he owned, I'm confident, so that he would be equipped to deal with the folly of the world, and mistook them for books of wisdom. I remember reading through (thankfully, at that young age, I wasn't smart enough to get truly poisoned by this nonsense) my father's books written by Sigmund Freud. I remember taking *On the Interpretation of Dreams* to bed with me and reading into the wee hours. I read *Civilization and Its Discontents*, finding myself horribly discontented with it. I thought psychoanalysis would equip me with wisdom, and proved myself to be a fool.

Perhaps worse than looking for wisdom in all the wrong places is looking for wisdom for all the wrong reasons. I sought out wisdom as a means to an end. I was not driven by a love of wisdom, but by a love of self. I wanted wisdom for what it could do for my ego. (What I really needed was a stronger super-ego to keep me in check.) I was more interested in seeming to be wise than I was in being wise. I wanted to establish a reputation among my peers as being a source for wisdom. I wanted to be a teenage sage. And so I became sophomoric, a wise fool. I looked for wisdom in ponderous lyrics from obtuse rock bands. Indeed, at that age I might have defined wisdom precisely as the ability to say ponderous things and to think ponderous thoughts. I was proud when I should have been ashamed.

James, a book some have suggested is the New Testament book of wisdom, begins with the beginning of wisdom. James writes his letter not as the brother of our Lord. He does not begin by affirming his role as the bishop of Jerusalem. He does not remind his readers that he presided over the first ecumenical council, the Jerusalem gathering recorded in Acts 15. No, he begins the revelation of God's wisdom by wisely affirming the real ground of his standing, that he is a "servant of God and of the Lord Jesus Christ" (1:1). Wisdom not only will not make us great before men, but will cause us to flee such carnal desires. Wisdom tells us, after all, that the first will be last. James writes wisely as one consumed with the fear of God, which is the beginning of wisdom (Prov. 9:10). And we do not fear God unless or until we believe God.

A PROMISE PRISTINE IN PLAINNESS

It was in the first few verses of James that I first came face to face with my own foolish refusal to believe the promises of God. Here God gives us a promise so pristine in its plainness that no amount of interpretive gymnastics will allow us to escape its plain meaning or its prodigal promise. James moves from his calling as a bondservant to encouraging his readers to count trials as all joy, to see the blessing in the hardships God sends our way. This, he tells us, will cause us to be complete, lacking in nothing. Then comes this shocking promise: "If any of you lacks wisdom, let him ask God, who gives generously to all without reproach, and it will be given him" (v. 5).

Is this not too much? Do we not cringe that God would make such a promise? He seems almost like a used-car salesman, promising us that the model we are looking at was only driven to church each week by a little old lady, then adding that it runs on water and gold comes out the exhaust. We are virtually offended at the crassness of the promise. We don't want to find ourselves put in a position where we have to affirm this text, which on its face sounds like magic. We are embarrassed by this almost as much as we are embarrassed by God telling us He made the world in six days. If we believe this promise as it is stated, we fear, all the world will think us fools. I mean, a surface reading of the text seems to suggest that a person could acquire wisdom simply by asking God for it, as if God were some sort of wisdom vending machine. So we set about reducing this promise down to something manageable and appropriate for skeptical modern ears.

Wisdom, we are told here, comes not by reading the right books. It is not gained by learning one's lessons in the school of hard knocks. Wisdom isn't the end result of a careful study of the history of philosophy. And we certainly don't get it by listening to aging rock stars. According to the Bible, we get wisdom by asking for it, by prayer. Our inability to believe the promises of God may grow out of our prior inability to believe in the power of prayer. We will look at other promises related to prayer in the coming chapters, but for now, let us consider the question we have all wrestled with since we were children—why do I receive some things I ask for in prayer but not others?

The answer may lie in the question. That is, what distinguishes positively answered prayer from negatively answered prayer may not be to whom we pray but that for which we ask. If we pray, along with Janis Joplin, "Lord, won't you buy me a Mercedes-Benz?" we can have a fairly high level of confidence that the Almighty's answer will be "No." If, however, we pray that Jesus will come back, while we may be asked to pray with patience, we can pray with confidence, for He has promised that He will return. When we ask for the Mercedes, we ought to include in our prayer the wisdom of Jesus as He faced His passion, "Yet not what I will, but what you will" (Mark 14:36b). When we pray for the return of Jesus, we need not add, "Yet not what I will, but what you will," for the Father has told us already that it is His will that Jesus would return. If we want our prayers answered positively, we would be wise to pray what He has promised. This is why James tells us that God gives to all liberally. We can expect God to shower us with a positive answer to this request precisely because wisdom is what He wants from us; it is what He calls us to. He is about the business of remaking us into the image of His Son, who is the express image of His glory, and who is likewise personified as wisdom in the Proverbs.

We are not yet like Him, however. We are still sinners and still doubters. That may be why we (happily?) cling to what follows as our tool for reducing this promise down to something manageable. James goes on to tell us, "But let him ask in faith, with no doubting . . ." (v. 6). It seems it's not just as simple as asking. If we want to get wisdom, we have to ask in a particular way, in faith, with no doubting. Well, where do we get this faith and how do we keep from doubting? Though James does not directly answer those questions here, I have a suggestion. Might it not be wise to ask God, who gives to all liberally and without reproach? He gave us our very start in faith and has nurtured us in our faith. Perhaps He might give us the faith to believe this promise. Perhaps, as we ask for wisdom from His hand, we might also pray with wisdom as one man did, "I believe; help my unbelief!" (Mark 9:24b). This man's prayer is a prayer *of* belief even as it is a prayer *for* belief. That is, it begins with belief, and believing, looks to the right source for relief of unbelief. We ask our heavenly Father for the faith to believe His promises. Believing His promises, we ask that they be fulfilled, that He would give us the blessing of wisdom.

How can we know whether God has answered this prayer positively?

Later in his epistle, James helps us learn to recognize what true wisdom looks like:

> Who is wise and understanding among you? By his good conduct let him show his works in the meekness of wisdom. But if you have bitter jealousy and selfish ambition in your hearts, do not boast and be false to the truth. This is not the wisdom that comes down from above, but is earthly, unspiritual, demonic. For where jealousy and selfish ambition exist, there will be disorder and every vile practice. But the wisdom from above is first pure, then peaceable, gentle, open to reason, full of mercy and good fruits, impartial and sincere. And a harvest of righteousness is sown in peace by those who make peace. (James 3:13–18)

MEEKNESS MAKES NO ARGUMENT

Our meekness begins in the face of the Word of God. When God speaks, do we argue with Him? Do we seek to twist His words into something reasonable? Or do we, believing like children, step out of the boat and begin to walk on water? Meekness responds to the Word of God with nothing other than a compliant and joyful, "Yes, sir." As we argued with the promise that we are made His children, we are not meek if we "humbly" argue with the God of all creation: "I know Your Word says You will give us wisdom if we will but ask You for it. But Lord, I am not worthy of such a promise. I am not owed wisdom simply because I ask for it. It's a nice promise and all, but really, I'm too humble to accept."

A month or so ago, I hired a young man who is a member of the church where I serve to do some work for me. Not being well myself, I asked him to cut a fallen tree or two into firewood for my family. This

young man usually works with his father, but he set aside half a day to do
this work for my family. When he arrived, we discovered that my chainsaw
wasn't in good enough shape to do the job. I paid the young man and took
him home. He was a touch uncomfortable taking pay for half a day's work
when he hadn't been able to work that long. I explained to him that I was
paying him for setting aside the time he had, and that it was my fault,
not his, that my tools weren't up to the task. He argued some more, and I
patiently tried to explain to him how unfair it would have been for me not
to pay him. I saw him a few days later, and he was still wanting to explain
why I was in the wrong. Every word out of his mouth was made with the
utmost respect (in fact, I know of few young men more gifted at treating
others with honor and dignity). So it wasn't his tone that began to wear on
my patience, but his unwillingness to give up the argument. I finally came
up with a shortcut that put an end to the discussion. I told him, "Jonathan, honor your elder." And that was that. God says that if we ask for
wisdom, He will give it to us. And that is that. Meekness before the face of
God submits to His Word, no matter how astonishing its promises. One
could argue that this is the very root of the shock of the promise. That is,
wisdom will come down from heaven as God's gift only if we recognize
that it can come down from heaven only as God's gift. We cannot earn
wisdom, but must receive it as a gift, as children.

We can know that we have received wisdom from above, the text tells
us, if our wisdom is not marked by bitter envy and self-seeking. The greater
problem evidenced in my snooping around my father's library as a teenager
wasn't that I was fool enough to think I could gain wisdom from Freud and
his ilk, but that I was fool enough to think that wisdom was a tool by which
I could gain glory. I treated wisdom the way Simon the sorcerer treated the
power of the Holy Spirit (Acts 8:14–24).

This kind of wisdom does far more than merely fail. This may be the
second-most-astonishing truth in this most astonishing passage: "Where

jealousy and selfish ambition exist, there will be disorder and every vile practice." Here is how we practice the folly of simultaneous translation with this text—we take these words and morph them into this: "Envy and self-seeking are bad." Now, one would be hard-pressed to take from this text any notion that envy and self-seeking are good, but there is rather much more to be learned here than that envy and self-seeking are merely bad. James tells us that where we see these things, envy and self-seeking, we will see not only confusion (it is interesting that we think confusion is the result of insufficient information; James tells us it is the result of insufficient sanctification) but every evil thing. *Every evil thing.* Envy and self-seeking are the very keys to Pandora's Box. If you have envy and self-seeking, do not be surprised if you likewise have idolatry, false worship, blasphemy, self-righteousness, rebellion, hatred, infidelity, theft, slander, and lust. From the opposite perspective, when we are dealing with these sins, we can rest assured that at bedrock what we have is envy and self-seeking.

Wisdom from above gives off a different aroma. It has the smell of beauty. It is pure, peaceable, gentle, willing to yield, full of mercy and good fruits, without partiality and without hypocrisy. It is unalloyed with selfishness and pride. It seeks out peace rather than strife, for blessed are the peacemakers. It is gentle rather than haughty, willing to yield, rather than insisting on its own way. It is full of mercy. Wisdom, after all, remembers our frame. It remembers that always, "There but for the grace of God go I." It not only bears good fruit, but *is* good fruit. See how very much the distinguishing marks of wisdom from above reflect the nature of the fruit of the Spirit. This should not surprise us, as they have the same source. Wisdom from above is without partiality. It is not interested in winning arguments or in protecting those whom we deem to be "on our side." Rather, it seeks to look at the world, as much as possible and appropriate, from God's perspective.

SEEING THE WORLD WITH GOD'S EYES

That is the very nature of wisdom, to see the world the way God sees the world. As we grow in wisdom, we learn more and more that the world does not exist for our glory, our comfort, our peace. We learn that it exists for God's glory. As we grow in wisdom, we learn more and more that God loves those who are His in Christ and that He is our Father. We learn to see our brothers the way our Father sees our brothers, as His adopted children in Christ. As we grow in wisdom, we learn more and more that there is no greater glory than the glory of Christ, and so we long for nothing more than to become more and more like Him. We learn to long for the pearl of great price rather than the foolish baubles of power, prestige, and plenty. As we grow in wisdom, we learn more and more that all that comes to pass in our lives comes to pass that we might grow in grace and wisdom. We learn, in short, the wisdom of counting it all joy, because the trials we fall into test our faith, and such produces patience. This patience in turn does its perfect work, making us complete, lacking nothing (James 1:2–4.) This patience reshapes us into the image of the Son, who is the express image of the Father.

This is wisdom, that we would know enough of our Father in heaven to actually believe that He is our Father in heaven. He delights to give us every good gift, and precious few gifts are greater than the gift of wisdom. When we come asking for the bread of wisdom, He does not give us the stone of folly. When we come asking for the egg of wisdom, He does not give us the serpent of folly. He loves us, with an unchanging and almighty love. He has promised to remake us into the image of His Son, who is wisdom in the flesh. This promise, then, isn't only for spiritual giants. It is not the domain of obtuse sages alone. It is not merely a gift that comes from unfathomable hardships. It is instead the bread of life, given to all who ask for it in faith. It is for me, for my wife, and for my children, from the oldest to the youngest.

Here, then, is wise counsel. Believe James, and so believe the Holy Spirit. It is both of them who have made this promise. Ask of your Father, that He would give you wisdom. If your asking is hampered by your unbelief, ask your Father to help you to believe. And if you have a hard time believing that He would help you with your unbelief, ask your Father to help you believe that He would help you believe. Keep walking backward in this manner until you cease to cry out in despair and begin to giggle in gospel joy. You see, when you asked for wisdom, He said, "I'd be happy to give you wisdom." And when you asked for greater faith, He said, "I'd be happy to give you greater faith." And when you asked Him for greater faith to believe that He would give you greater faith, He said, "I'd be happy to give you greater faith." And when you finally started laughing, He had been laughing already, because He loves you. It is His story, after all, and we are players on His stage.

If, in His grace, this gift of wisdom from time to time should be a help to your friends, and if they should give thanks to you for your wisdom, tell them where you got it. Tell them how you got it. And tell them there is an endless supply there for them as well. All they have to do is ask. Our Father gives to all liberally and without reproach.

CHAPTER FIVE

CHILDREN ARE A HERITAGE

PSALM 127

About eight hours from now, I will be sitting down to teach a Bible study. That study will be quite a challenge for me, but probably an even greater challenge for those in attendance. I am in the midst of a series of studies on the sovereignty of God. Each of my talks is based on a chapter from my book *Almighty Over All*. The sovereignty of God is almost always difficult for folks to deal with, but tonight I will consider the relationship between the sovereignty of God and the fall of man. I will attempt to answer the question of how Adam and Eve, created good, could fall into sin.

I first addressed this issue publicly at a conference nearly a dozen years ago. I titled my lecture, "Something Wicked This Way Comes." After I gave my answer to this great puzzle and had said all I had to say, I was surprised to find that I still had ten minutes of my allotted time left. I suggested to the audience, "Having answered the problem of evil in the last fifty minutes, I will take the next ten minutes to solve the mystery of the Trinity."

There are different kinds of hard questions. The Trinity, while a great mystery, isn't something people are apt to get offended over. Few people have a deep commitment to one view as against another (though perhaps they should). The origin of evil, on the other hand, is both a great mystery and something apt to raise hackles. While I'm not smart enough to untie any real theological Gordian knots, I tend to not shy away from issues that get people hot under the collar. I'm at ease encouraging people to face hard truths of the Bible. I have spoken before on the reality and nature of hell. I have written on the current use of imprecatory psalms, those passages in which the psalmist beseeches God to send judgment against the wicked. If you need someone to stand firm on a hard truth, I'm always willing to volunteer.

Another great mystery is that people sometimes have a harder time accepting biblical promises of blessing than they do biblical promises of cursing. One would think that when God makes us a promise of blessing that we would be most eager to believe it. One would think that we would have to be warned about reading the fine print rather than trying to add fine print ourselves. The Devil, however, is a crafty being. He is not merely interested in enticing us to find pleasure in illicit places. He likewise wants us to miss the pleasures that God has offered us. His fiendish delight is to rob us of our joy. He understands far better than we do that a failure to believe God, whether it is about the circumstances leading up to the fall of man, about the nature of the Trinity, or about His promises, is sin.

A SERIES OF SMALL STEPS

The promise we are about to cover is one my dear wife and I came to embrace through some small steps. I began, like most modern evangelicals, believing that God had blessed the church with the gift of birth control. God has given us work to do. He calls us to subdue the earth, to make manifest the reign of Christ over all things. One thing the Christian will never do is find himself with nothing to do. So wasn't God good and wise to bless us with the technology we need to limit the size of our families so we can be about His work? We have worlds to remake, cultures to reconstruct. Children, we seem to believe, can get in the way. (Please keep in mind that, as common as my former view is, historically speaking, it is an anomaly. Virtually every professing Christian, up until some time in the mid-twentieth century, believed it sinful to use birth control.)

Our first step away from this common view happened when we came to understand that birth control was, on its face, "unnatural." Such a conviction, however much it might make us uncomfortable, doesn't give us a clear "Thou shalt not. . . ." A particular behavior being "unnatural" doesn't quite reach that standard. As I struggled with this, I contacted an acquaintance, a Roman Catholic professor at a Jesuit university. I wanted to understand the reasoning behind Rome's rejection of "unnatural" family planning and acceptance of "natural" family planning. He explained to me the depth of the unnaturalness of using contraceptives. He did not affirm that the marital act existed solely for the procreation of children. He did explain that food does not exist solely for the purpose of providing fuel for the body. God in His grace bestowed on the marital act the aspect of pleasure, even as He bestowed on our daily bread the aspect of delightful tastes. Using contraceptives, my friend said, was akin to the practice of the ancient Romans at their feasts, wherein they would fill themselves with food, only to purge that food from their bodies so that they might eat more. Just as bulimia separates what God has brought together, the taking in of fuel and the joy of good food, so contraception separates procreation from the joy of the marital act.

My wife and I took another step on this issue when we came face to face with a rather clear "Thou shalt not. . . . It wasn't a clear prohibition on family planning. Instead it was a clear prohibition on marital abstinence. Paul tells us, "Do not deprive one another, except perhaps by agreement for a limited time, that you may devote yourselves to prayer" (1 Cor. 7:5a). There is certainly a biblical warrant for times of extended abstinence among married couples. Avoiding the blessing of children, however, isn't among the reasons listed.

At this point, my wife and I determined to obey God in this area of our lives. We did not want to act unnaturally and we did not want to deprive one another. In addition, we had a rather significant "Thou shalt . . ." encouraging us on this path. In the garden, God commanded Adam and Eve to be fruitful and to multiply, to fill the earth (Gen. 1:28a). That settled the issue for us.

Or so we thought. It was the last step in our thinking that was the most dramatic, that required the greatest amount of faith. This last step might seem at first blush to have been a step away from the direction we were heading. At this point in our lives, we were not willing to say that the practice of birth control is a sin. What we were willing to say instead was and is far more radical—children are a blessing sent from God.

THE ANTINOMIANISM OF THE LEGALISTS

We can get at the difference between these two affirmations by looking to how Jesus approached the law in His Sermon on the Mount. Among other important things, one of the messages Jesus communicated to His audience on the Mount was about the antinomianism of the legalists. We tend to think of antinomians and legalists as being on opposite ends of the spectrum. Legalists are those, like the Pharisees, who like to add to God's law, placing burdens on the people of God that God has not placed on them. (I suspect many of you think you are reading a legalist, if not a Pharisee, due to my uncommon views on birth control.) Antinomians, on the other hand, are those who denigrate or reduce the law of God (*anti* meaning "against" and *nomos* meaning "law"). How then can one be both a legalist and an antino-mian? The Pharisees managed it quite well. Legalists tend to add to the law rules that are relatively easy to keep. If, for instance, we were to affirm that dancing is sinful, then we would give up dancing and move on with our lives. But antinomians tend to diminish God's law at the very places we are tempted. As legalists, we suggest it is a sin to dance; as antinomians, we gloss over the sin of pride that we commit because, unlike others, we don't dance.

In the Sermon on the Mount, Jesus informs us that the law is not quite as discreet as the Pharisees had led the people to believe. He says, "You have heard that it was said to those of old, 'You shall not murder, and whoever murders will be liable to judgment.' But I say to you that everyone who is angry with his brother will be liable to judgment" (Matt. 5:21–22a). In like manner, Jesus explains, "You have heard that it was said, 'You shall not com-mit adultery.' But I say to you that whoever looks at a woman with lustful intent has already committed adultery with her in his heart" (vv. 27–28). The law includes more than simple, clear-cut prohibitions; it includes sins we commit in the privacy of our hearts and minds. Subsumed under the law against murder is the law against unjust anger; subsumed under the law against adultery is the law against lusting in one's heart.

God doesn't prohibit unjust anger merely because He is interested in protecting life. Instead, He does it because human life is a great good. When God says our failure to do x is a sin, He is affirming at the same time that to do x is good. Alternately, if God says doing y is a sin, He is giving a cor-responding call to do non-y. I would suggest that we not only must not kill, but must protect life. Further, we not only must protect life, we must cherish it, delight in it.

This contrast is highlighted in our text, the promise we have been given:

Unless the LORD builds the house,

those who build it labor in vain.
Unless the LORD watches over the city,
the watchman stays awake in vain.
It is in vain that you rise up early
and go late to rest,
eating the bread of anxious toil;
for he gives to his beloved sleep.

Behold, children are a heritage from the LORD,
the fruit of the womb a reward.
Like arrows in the hand of a warrior,
are the children of one's youth.
Blessed is the man who fills his quiver with them!
He shall not be put to shame
when he speaks with his enemies in the gate. (Ps. 127)

Derek Kidner, in his commentary on the Psalms, makes the observation that some have argued that this psalm brings together two distinct poems, so great is the seeming divide between the first and second halves. Solomon begins by discussing issues of security. Neither homes nor cities can rest secure if God is not protecting them. Solomon affirms that it is not our efforts that bring us safety, but the gracious oversight of God that does so. Having made this point, the psalm seems to suddenly turn and begins talking about children.

Kidner helps us see the connection by directing our attention to Genesis 11. This chapter begins with the story of the Tower of Babel. Here we see the people building in an attempt to make a lasting name and to provide security. These things are pursued without the blessing of God. They end up in utter calamity. The chapter ends, however, with the story of Terah. He is given a son, Abraham. From there the blessings have been poured out ever since.

WORRIES ABOUT HOMES AND SECURITY

It is telling that it is often our worries about our homes and our security that encourage us not to see children as a blessing. How, we wonder, if we do not take measures to avoid more children, will we ever provide for those we have? How shall we be secure if our homes are invaded by little children who are so dependent on us? Just as it was foolish for the builders of the Tower of Babel to seek their security in bricks and mortar (while they refused to obey God's command to fill the earth), so it was wise for Terah to seek his security in the blessing of God, specifically in the blessing of children. Here the two themes come together. It is God who builds and protects cities, just as it is God who opens and closes the womb. It is only through His sovereign power that we are protected, and it is through that same power that we are blessed. We worry about our houses and He blesses our homes.

God, therefore, is not merely telling us the right thing to *do*; He is telling us the right thing to *want*. He tells us that children are a heritage, a reward, arrows, and a blessing. *Heritage* is not a word we're terribly used to. It is akin to a legacy, something we typically hear about as a president nears the end of his tenure. Pundits wonder about what a president's "legacy" will be, how he will be remembered once he has left office. I understand something of what this is like, the temptation to look for a "heritage" in all the wrong places. Having a father who is well-known in certain circles, one who is widely read and respected, it is difficult for me not to measure my value as a man by those standards. I have inherited a peculiar view of what it means to be a godly man, and thus I find it difficult not to conclude that my measure as a man is the number of people who look to me as a teacher of the Bible or listen to me on the radio.

The Bible, however, tells of a different standard. It tells me that my children are my heritage. My reputation is measured by their character, not my "career." While this is a challenge to me as I look at myself, I see the principle clearly in others. One of the regular aspects of the work I do is speaking at conferences. To speak well, it is fairly important to get a sense of the audience to whom one is speaking. As I seek, as much as is possible, to get a sense of those who have gathered, my standards are not the quality of the cars in the parking lot or the sophistication of the dress of those in attendance. Instead, I look into the faces of the wives and children. If I find joy there, I know I have gathered with godly men who are leading godly families.

I went through a time not long ago when my reputation took a rather serious hit. It was a difficult time for me, but even more so for my wife. My skin is relatively thick, but she stands by her man. She takes attacks on me as attacks on herself. I sought to comfort her and myself by reminding her of a biblical truth. "Dear," I told her, "we don't need to be worrying about this. My life's work is nothing other than you and our children." A gold watch is not a heritage. A name on a plaque is not a heritage. Children, according to the Word of God, are a heritage. Every other ounce of energy I spend may end up having been poured into wood, hay, and stubble. My children, on the other hand, one way or another, will last into eternity.

The psalmist also tells us that children are a reward. This may make us more theologically uncomfortable than financially uncomfortable. How did we, sinners that we are, find ourselves in a position to receive rewards? By His grace. Whatever rewards we might receive, we receive them not as our due but by grace. Rewards from the hand of God are grace upon grace, God crowning His own crowns. None of this changes the nature of children. They are still a reward to us. Here again, we come face to face with that last and most vital step on this issue. We do not begrudgingly leave the size of our families in God's hand, because He says children are a reward and it would be insulting to the Giver for us to say, "No, thank you." Rather, we are to actually believe God, that when He blesses us with children they are actual blessings. They are a gift, a plus, a cause for joy.

We might see this clearly if we would learn to compare apples to apples. I first made this point with a fine, godly older woman. I was a friend of this great saint and of her daughter. The mom, knowing I was a friend of her daughter, and hoping I might talk some sense into the younger lady, complained to me about how many children her daughter had had. She thought her daughter was compromising her health by bearing and caring for so many children. I knew the older woman well enough to know that her care and concern for her daughter were genuine, as was her love for her grandchildren. So I asked the older saint, "Which one of your grandchildren would you like to give back?" Our tendency is to look at more children as just that, more children. But God doesn't give us number three or number four or number five. Instead, He gives us Shannon and Delaney and Erin Claire, which is a whole other matter. (And He thus far has blessed my family not with six and seven, but with Maili and Reilly.)

GUARDING AGAINST FALSE CONNECTIONS

Recognizing that children are a blessing and reward, however, we need to include at least one caveat. Because God moves us from grace to grace, we want to avoid the mistake that Job's friends made. They argued that because suffering and sin have some kind of connection, it therefore was possible to measure a man's sin by the amount of suffering that man went through. In like manner, while the Bible says that children are a reward, this does not mean that one can measure the level of favor one has with God by the number of smiling faces in the family Christmas picture. Prosperity is also described as a blessing from God's hand, as a reward, but only the most crass health-and-wealth huckster would argue that there is a one-to-one relationship between a man's righteousness and his bank account. God says children are a reward. We are fools if we don't believe Him. Believing Him, however, doesn't mean God will necessarily bless you with a dozen children. It simply means that if

He did, it would be cause for celebration. Children in the Christian home are a locus of joy, and so should be treated that way.

The psalmist then describes children as arrows. The psalm begins by warning us that only God is capable of guarding a city and ends by affirming not that children *need* protection in our homes but that they *are* a protection in our homes. Arrows defend our homes, but they also are offensive weapons used to attack the enemy. Children keep us safe, but they likewise go forth as soldiers of the Lord. They keep us safe in at least this manner—they encourage us toward humility. They keep us grounded, focused on eternal matters rather than the relatively trivial issues that consume the busy world around us. Sadly, too many kingdom-minded people miss this point. They are rightly zealous about bringing all things under the subjection of Christ. They rightly recognize that our calling is to expand the borders where Christ's lordship is affirmed. But they wrongly choose a worldly path to world conquest. Some argue that we should not seek to receive the full blessing of children from God's hand so that we can make our children better culture warriors. That is, we need to have fewer children so we can pour more of ourselves into them, and more of our resources. With only a few children, we will be able to send them to the finest schools in preparation for sending them to the finest universities. From there, they will become power brokers in the broader culture, and so make known the reign of Christ. It's a nice theory, but the psalmist doesn't say that highbrow diplomas are arrows in our hands. He doesn't argue that positions of power are arrows for battle. Instead, he tells us that *children* are arrows.

That said, there is a danger on the other side of the equation, particularly among homeschooling families. Too many of us, again rightly wanting to make known the reign of Christ over all things and rightly seeing children as weapons in our warfare, end up turning children into a means to an end. Rather than seeking to raise up godly seed so that they can clean up the broader culture, we must understand that our children *are* the culture, that to sanctify them is the goal, the end for which we exist.

The bottom line is this: children are a blessing to those who belong to Christ. If we believe this, we will not seek to have more children because we see that it is a sin to avoid them. We will not, with stiff upper lips, do our gospel duty and have children, as unpleasant as that may be. No, to be open to God's blessing, and in turn to receive that blessing, is to walk into joy. It is to enjoy the good life. Kidner walked in wisdom when he affirmed in his commentary on Psalms 73–150 (InterVarsity, 1975), "God's gifts are as unpretentious as they are miraculous."

We need not, in order to do great things for the kingdom of God, spend year after year acquiring advanced degrees in order to acquire a following. We need not, in order to do great things for the kingdom of God, acquire specialized gifts and talents in order to make our way in the world. We need not, in order to do great things for the kingdom of God, tax our brains to come up with some grand power scheme. We need not, in order to do great things for the kingdom of God, set aside every joy and pleasure. Instead, the gift of children is a gift that nearly anyone can receive. These arrows are weapons with which nearly anyone can be blessed.

What might happen if we believed this? We can speculate and guess all day long. We can note that the Bible also teaches us that those who hate God love death, and therefore joyful acceptance of God's blessing combined with faithful nurture of God's covenant children might make a better world. We can do some astounding math, imagining what would happen should God bless each of us with seven children, and each of our children with seven children, and each of their children with seven children, and so daydream about a glorious future. All of this may be perfectly appropriate. Without such speculation, however, we can safely conclude this: if we believed this glorious promise of God, we might stop saying "no" to Him and His gifts. And if that happened, the next thing you know, we might just be blessed, rewarded. We might just enjoy the joy of children.

After "I love you," each of my children hears this from me more than anything else: "You are a joy in Daddy's life." This is not a conclusion I reached by faith, by believing what my eyes could not see. This is instead a conclusion I reached by experience, by enjoying what my heart could not miss. God is true, and too many men are liars. He has promised to bless us. We would be not only wise but happy if we were to believe Him. May God make you, your children, and your children's children fruitful.

CHAPTER SIX

THE DESIRES OF YOUR HEART

PSALM 37:4

The Serpent, as we have already considered, has more tricks in his bag than simply trying to allure us with illicit pleasures. Though there is nothing new under the sun, his stratagems are myriad. Remember that he does not run in fear when we open our Bibles, but instead trains us in the diabolical art of simultaneous translation.

One of the key supports to this practice is what sociologists call "plausibility structures." These are realities about a culture or subculture that, through no intention of those realities, make certain propositions or convictions seem more plausible to those inside that culture or subculture. Consider, for instance, toothpaste. Toothpaste has no desire to see the world embrace some sort of relativistic worldview. It has no hard commitment to the notion that we all can construct our own realities. It really doesn't care. A world, however, wherein it is "normal" for us to be able to choose from among twenty brands, six flavors, and eight sizes of toothpaste is a world wherein choice seems natural. It is all too easy for us to believe that because we can choose from among all these varieties of toothpaste, with none being the right or wrong answer, that we also ought to be able to choose to believe whatever we like about reality, or perhaps more important, morality. Because we are gods in the grocery aisle, we think ourselves gods in general.

Toothpaste is not the only thing to shape our thinking. What might you guess if I were to ask you to name the most world-changing invention of the past five hundred years? Some of you no doubt would conclude that the computer, like the one I am using right now, would have to be it. Others might guess that it's the automobile or the television. Paul Johnson, in his outstanding work *The Birth of the Modern*, made his case for road-paving technology as a critical linchpin into the modern world. We could spend hours debating the issue. My suggestion isn't anything as grand as the computer. Instead, I'd suggest that we consider that piece of machinery that rests on our wrists. It may be that the personal timepiece is the most world-changing creation of the last half-millennium. In the same way that the telegraph created the notion of news (see Neil Postman's *Amusing Ourselves to Death* for a compelling discussion on this), so did the personal timepiece create the notion of time.

Of course, time, as well as the notion of time, existed long before the personal timepiece. Before timepieces, we were apt to measure our lives by seasons and days rather than hours and minutes. Progress or regress, in like manner, had to be measured in smaller steps, or bigger chunks, depending on how you look at it. Timepieces gave us the ability to measure not just time in greater detail, but the speed at which we are reaching or falling behind our goals. Because we now can measure progress, we are all the more concerned with our ability to progress. That, in turn, leads to worry. We worry that the world is not as it should be, because we think we must make it as it should be. What we need, however, is a bigger vision, a view of time that transcends not only minutes and hours, but days and seasons. When we see the bigness of time, we can be at peace.

David gets at this broader perspective in Psalm 37, which begins:

> Fret not yourself because of evildoers;
> be not envious of wrongdoers!
> For they shall soon fade like the grass
> and wither like the green herb. (vv. 1–2)

When we step back from looking at the world from the perspective of second by second, we can begin to see the judgment against the wicked. As we live above time, we witness the reality that it is not the children of God but the wicked who are like the grass; they come and they go.

Later in the psalm, we see the same theme repeated about the wicked, while a grand promise is made to those who are in Christ:

> Be still before the LORD and wait patiently for him;
> fret not yourself over the one who prospers in his way,
> over the man who carries out evil devices!
>
> Refrain from anger, and forsake wrath!
> Fret not yourself; it tends only to evil.
> For the evildoers shall be cut off,
> but those who wait for the LORD shall inherit the land . . .
> and delight themselves in abundant peace. (vv. 7–11)

Here is a promise that Jesus picked up in His Sermon on the Mount, wherein we are told that the meek will inherit the earth. We are commanded here not to worry, but to have the faith that God will bring judgment against the wicked, and that we will inherit the earth and delight ourselves in the abundance of peace.

As grand as this promise is (and please do not listen to the Devil as he seeks to get you to translate this into something safe: "Oh, this is just a figure of speech. It's not like you'll actually inherit the earth."), it is not the focus of this chapter. As glorious and shocking as it is that we will delight ourselves in the abundance of peace, the promise I'd like us to consider is found in verse 4, where we read:

> Delight yourself in the LORD,
> And he will give you the desires of your heart.

A cursory reading of this promise may cause us to be taken aback. Does this say what we think it says? Does God promise to give us whatever our heart desires? When we looked at God's promise to give wisdom to those who would ask it of Him (chap. 4), we noted our desire to cover for God. We suggested that He seemed to have gotten carried away with His own marketing copy and had overpromised. Here the promise may be grander still, but thankfully He had the sense this time to include, right in the text, the weasel words that make this promise much more palatable.

SEEING THROUGH THE "WEASEL WORDS"

Though it hardly sounds professional, "weasel words" is an expression common among professional marketing writers. Too often, advertisers are sophists, manipulators of words and emotions. Consider, for a moment, the transparent but apparently effective practice of pricing. When you discover that a pizza is available for $5.99, the pizza company is trying to get your mind to think $5 while it is trying to empty your wallet of $6. The pricing structure is aimed at convincing you to think one thing while doing another. Weasel words work in the same way. Those who use them want your heart to see and latch onto the promise, all while avoiding actually making the promise, lest they find themselves outside the law, charged with false advertising.

Suppose, for instance, that the publishers of this book were to advertise it this way: "May be the greatest book written in the past three hundred years." Is it possible that you are reading the greatest book written in the past three hundred years? While I am happy to concede that such is terribly unlikely, perhaps on par with a person hitting eighteen holes in one in a single round of golf, it still remains a possibility. But such marketing copy, without committing to the notion that the book is that good, at least has induced the reader to begin to think in those terms through the use of the weasel words "may be."

Weasel words are so common in our day that we are adept at finding them. And they certainly are readily apparent in our text. We don't spend long hours daydreaming about all the great goodies God will bring us because of His promise to give us the desires of our hearts; rather, we are quickly brought up short by the qualifier. Before we get the desires of our heart, we must delight ourselves in the Lord. There go our dreams, up in smoke. The string attached to the promise may as well be a noose. We're not going to see the promise fulfilled. We believe, I believe, that we cannot meet this qualifier because we can't begin to understand it.

I come from a long line of Presbyterians. We Presbyterians are rather gifted at careful exposition of our beliefs. We are a creedal branch of the church, given to point-by-point, proposition-by-proposition, proof-text-by-proof-text theological affirmations. Our most simple formulation, constructed during the English Reformation, is the Westminster Shorter Catechism. This is a list of 107 simple questions and 107 profound answers, used principally to teach sound doctrine to children and new believers. The first question, however, is more teleological than theological. It addresses the great question of our purpose, our reason for being. It asks, "What is the chief end of man?" It answers, "Man's chief end is to glorify God, and to enjoy him forever."

Presbyterians have, or so we think, a pretty good idea of what it means to glorify God. We affirm that God is glorified as we turn to His Son for our redemption. He is glorified as we strive to obey all that He has commanded. He is glorified through the proclamation of the gospel. He is glorified as we gather together in corporate worship in His honor and as we worship Him as families during the week. He is glorified when we reflect the glory of His creative work by being about the business of exercising dominion over the creation. We could expound for hours on what it means to glorify God, making the mistake of believing that even such expounding glorifies Him. Our problem is found in the last phrase to the catechism answer. "Glorify God" we think we understand, but what is this about enjoying Him?

Any talk about emotions tends to make Presbyterians a touch itchy. Considering joy just about gives us the hives. Enjoying God, to Presbyterian ears, sounds like something our charismatic brothers might do. Reformed folk aren't happy people; they are holy people. We don't want to enjoy things; we want to be on a quest. And we want to be uncomfortable all along the way. That's how we demonstrate our piety. We want to do the right thing, against all odds. Being burned at the stake appeals to us. Crossing vast oceans to start over in an untamed wilderness, that's more our speed.

It may well be that God's greatest challenge to people with my theological baggage is that we would learn to delight in Him. It may be that rejoicing in the Lord, more than suffering for the Lord, is the very peak of what sanctification is all about. If the divines who wrote the Westminster Shorter Catechism are right, this is what we were made for. Enjoying the glory of God is not merely something we ought to do, but is our very reason for being.

The fretting we are so prone to, that the psalmist warns us against, is the result of our propensity to look for joy in all the wrong places. We think we can rejoice when we are not surrounded by evildoers. We think we can rejoice when the workers of iniquity are suffering rather than celebrating. We think we can rejoice when our bank account is fat, when our job is secure, when our children receive their diplomas, when it doesn't rain on our picnic, when our football team wins the championship.

In short, we think our joy is circumstantial. And indeed it is. We should rejoice only in those circumstances in which we have the pearl of great price. When our reputations are being savaged, when our children suffer from serious illnesses, when our wives are going through chemotherapy, when the odometers on our cars turn over, again, then we remember that we gave up everything in order to receive the one thing that matters.

FINDING THROUGH DELIGHTING

This is how God's promise here once again becomes a real promise. This is how the words we thought were weasel words become in reality the very power of the promise. God is not telling us here that if we will do the good but difficult work of delighting ourselves in Him, then He will buy us all Mercedes-Benzes. The promise isn't that if you become sufficiently sanctified, then God will be like a genie in a bottle to you, granting you whatever you wish. Instead, the promise is this: that as we delight ourselves in the Lord, we discover that we already have the desire of our hearts. The Lord Himself is the desire of our hearts.

One could argue that all the promises we have looked at, and all that we will look at, boil down to this single promise. If we seek, we will find. If we knock, the door will be opened to us. We think that the only foolish way to handle this text is to turn it into a vending machine. We think only the extreme fringe of the health-and-wealth prophets miss the meaning of this text. How much worse are we, who come to this text and turn it into mere poetry?

As we delight ourselves in the Lord, we enter into the very power to put aside all the pettiness that consumes us. In our natural state, we do not merely live lives of quiet desperation, failing to escape the vanity of vanity. Our problem isn't merely that we can't find that which has meaning. Our problem is that we are attracted to, that we commit ourselves to, that we pursue vanity, chasing the wind. We seek meaning in the meaningless. But when we are disinterested in having a good reputation, losing it does not hurt us. When we are not consumed with good health, losing it does not cause us to stumble. When we do not seek earthly treasure, we do not despair when thieves or rust take it from us.

While I was in the midst of a lengthy series of trials, a younger pastor friend approached me with a question. "How do you manage," he asked, "to stay so 'up' after all that you've been through? What's the secret?"

I told him, "I have the one thing that I need."

He walked away puzzled, but soon returned with another question. "Isn't there anything you need?" he asked this time.

After a few seconds of thought, I suggested: "Yes, there is one thing I still need. I need God to help me better understand that I need nothing beyond the pearl of great price. When we delight ourselves in the Lord, we leave vanity and enter into meaning. We discover that He is not only the Promise Keeper, but that He is the Promise. He is our exceedingly great reward."

Easier said than done, isn't it? The fact that we enter into great joy and blessing when we believe the promises of God does not necessarily cause us to believe the promises of God. Our unbelief is the product of seeing with our eyes. Of course, it is our troubles that our eyes see. What we need to see is the greater reality. We believe the promises of God better when we are better able to see Him. His glory is enough. When the three disciples witnessed the glory of Christ revealed on the Mount of Transfiguration, they did not wonder whether fame or riches were better. They did not have to weigh that experience against any others to see which was more glorious. In order to delight in Him, we need to see Him, for He is the very essence of delight.

Many believe that there are levels of heaven, just as there are levels of hell. All those who enter into glory are filled with joy. No one there will ever be sad because he or she isn't sufficiently high up. How can these both be true? Some have compared this state of affairs to different-sized containers, each filled to the brim with joy. One who lives a life of debauchery until making a deathbed conversion might be a thimble full of joy as he enters into heaven. A person who lived a life of quiet faithfulness, on the other hand, might begin eternity as a fifty-five-gallon drum filled with joy. Each one is full; none has any lack. But some have more than others.

Another way to describe this reality takes its cue from 1 Corinthians 13:12a: "For now we see in a mirror dimly, but then face to face." Each of us, in heaven, will behold the glory of God. Some, however, according to those who believe in levels of heaven, will see that glory more clearly than others. All will be delighted by what they see, but some will see more than others. Here, however, we hold out hope that over time we will see more and more. Our eyes will grow more and more clear as more and more of the glory of God is revealed to us, into eternity. We will move eternally from grace to grace because we will see Him more and more.

SEEKING TO SEE HIS GLORY

But how can this happen on earth as it does in heaven? How can we, on this side of the veil, better see the glory of God? This pursuit ought to drive our every conviction, our every decision. We ought to be asking ourselves not, "Will a or b make me more happy?" but instead, "Will a or b help me to see Jesus more clearly?" When we make important life decisions—how we should educate our children or what our marriages should look like—the idea isn't to make the choice that will cause us to fit in best with our friends. Likewise, we ought not to choose the church we will attend based on which one has the programs we prefer or the most charming preacher. Instead, we need to seek to discern which will make known to us more of the glory of our Lord. As we raise our children, we do not make choices based on what we think will best prepare them to live "successful" lives, but what will best show them Jesus.

Jesus shows up in some of the strangest places, if we will but look. Not long ago, God blessed me with a vision of His glory. In His providence, I happened to look out a window. I saw outside, under a tree, two of my five daughters. Delaney, the six-year-old, was lying in the grass beside Erin Claire, the three-year-old. Both of them were perfectly at peace and at ease as Delaney read a story to her little sister. Please don't misunderstand. I'm not suggesting that Jesus is a little girl. I'm not embracing some sort of silly Eastern mysticism wherein Jesus is whatever you want Him to be. Neither am I suggesting, on the other hand, that all that happened here was that I witnessed a good thing, a mere gift from God for which I ought to give thanks. Instead, the very glory of God shone forth from these children. God revealed His character in this scene. It wasn't just good, it was Jesus.

God has blessed our family with a particularly potent revealer of His glory. Our daughter Shannon, who is about to turn ten as I write, has special needs. She cannot talk. She cannot feed herself. She cannot use the bathroom. What she can do, however, is embrace the glory of God all around her in a natural, unaffected way. She is free of the foolish conceit that suggests that sunlight is merely the result of a strange intersection of particle characteristics and wave characteristics set off by sundry forms of energy and moving at 186,000 miles per second. Instead, she sees sunlight for what it is, the very glory of God. She pats at it and laughs the laugh of the godly, that God should so manifest His glory. We, by His grace, behold His glory because we are allowed to watch her take in His glory.

Here is one more place where our Presbyterian austerity is a tool of the Devil. (Truth be told, the roots of our folly here are not so much Presbyterianism as modernism. The unbelievers have told us the universe is a self-made machine, and we think we have answered them because we believe it to be a machine made by God.) Awe and reverence are great things. We ought never to take the things of God lightly. Rather, as we take in the glory of God that the heavens declare, we ought to be humbled by His greatness. As great as awe and reverence are, however, sometimes giddiness is a fine response as well. We are seeing the glory of God when we can look at the snow descending and see there the laughter of God. We are seeing the glory of God when we can look up at the stars and see not flaming balls of simple chemicals but the dancing and singing heavenly host. As my poet friend Douglas Jones puts it:

> *The universe moves by loyalty.*
> *Righteousness and unrighteousness move material things,*
> *not matter pushing matter. . . .*
> *Loyalty makes plants grow.*
> *Love makes dough rise.* (*Credenda/Agenda*. Vol. 18, No. 4)

If we would learn to see the glory of God, we must first learn to see the glory of His creation. We must take our fingers out of our ears, that we might hear the music of the spheres.

It is not because we are sinners that we want to be happy, that we long for joy, that we want to live abundant lives. It is because we are sinners that we are not happy, that we miss out on joy, that our lives are impoverished. Because we are sinners, we look for these things, these good things, in all the wrong places. Jesus told us that He came to give us life, and life abundant (John 10:10). God has not merely offered us these things, He has not merely made them possible, He has promised them to us. He has provided these things for us in His Son. Our longings, He tells us in Psalm 37, will be met. Our hunger and thirst will be met. If we delight ourselves in the Lord, we will not merely have all that we could want, but will have more than we can imagine. If we delight ourselves in the Lord, He will give us the desires of our hearts. If we delight ourselves in the Lord, we will walk into the rest Augustine wrote of when he prayed, "Our hearts are restless, O Lord, until they find their rest in Thee."

When we fail to believe God, we are not set free to pursue joy and happiness, but are cut off from its source. When we fail to believe God, we become dry dust, withered grass. When we fail to believe God, we do not trade present pleasure for future pain, but embrace present emptiness and future agony. We will be cut down, cut off; we will be no more.

If we would believe God, we would see that He has not called us to austerity but to overflowing blessing. If we would believe God, we would taste not the dry dust of duty but the wine on the lees, and eat of the fat and marrow (Isa. 25:6). If we would believe God, our reputations would not be sour but raucous. If we would believe God, we would be blessed in the land He has given us and we would feed on His faithfulness. If we would believe God, we would inherit the earth. If we would believe God, we would receive the greatest blessing of all—we would see Him and be filled.

CHAPTER SEVEN

OPEN WINDOWS
OF HEAVEN

MALACHI 3:10

The Indians of the old West, we are told, were a resourceful bunch. When they killed a buffalo, they did not merely take home the tastiest portions and leave the rest to rot on the plains. Instead, they found uses for the hide, the bones, and the sinew. Even the horns were put to good use.

Likewise, the Devil is not only terribly crafty, but resourceful as well. His schemes are rarely discreet, operating on one level only, and with only one goal. When, for instance, he came up with the silly notion that there is no objective right and wrong, he was not merely seeking to confuse the gullible. That's all well and good, but there is more he can achieve through this strategy. For instance, actual Christians can lose a degree of confidence in the Bible. They may not embrace relativism, but they may feel intimidated by its general acceptance. Perhaps most subtle is this eventuality, which affects even the most ardent defenders of the biblical truth account: when we come to the Ten Commandments in Exodus 20, we are told what God really requires, objectively. But the Devil succeeds if we come to this text believing that its ultimate purpose is to refute relativism. The Ten Commandments do not merely tell us that there is an objective right and wrong. They do even more than tell us what that objective right and wrong are. We have missed the power of the Ten Commandments if we miss their exposition of the glory of God—if we miss the beauty of the calling He has placed on our lives.

The Devil has gotten much the same kind of mileage out of what has come to be known as the "health-and-wealth" gospel. This is a school of thought, far too common on "Christian" television, that holds that God's desire is for all His people to enjoy perfect health and astonishing wealth. Adherents of this view, sometimes called the "word-faith" movement, argue that their own lavish lifestyles are a sign of God's blessing on their lives and ministries. They argue in turn that others can be so blessed by giving generously to these ministries.

The Devil scores points when some people believe that God wills all of us to enjoy unlimited health and wealth. But many, if not all, of the proponents of this doctrine teach other grave heresies as well, and seduce the ignorant into those heresies. However, the Devil does not merely encourage adherents of this doctrine to embrace theological error. It isn't as if all that happens is that they misunderstand the nature of the Trinity. No, they are not only wrong about this doctrine and that, but are positively encouraged toward particular sins, such as covetousness and greed. As in Gordon Gekko's *Wall Street* world, greed in this worldview is good. This particular temptation is all the more potent, of course, when the "health-and-wealth" gospel "works." That is, those who find themselves enjoying material prosperity after having made their "faith pledge" are confirmed in their greed by that prosperity.

The craftiness and the economy of the Devil, however, really show up best when this approach to blessing doesn't "work." That is, when a person sends his pledge in to the health-and-wealth guru and nothing happens, it is all too likely that he will not blame the guru and his false message but instead will grow angry with God. He will become bitter because God did not keep a promise that God never actually made. That, for all its diabolical evil, is certainly efficient. The Devil has these poor folks coming and going.

The Devil, however, isn't done yet. It may well be that the greatest effect of the propagation of this foolishness isn't found among those who fall for it but among those who don't fall for it. In other words, the heresy is most effective among those who don't believe the heresy. Those who do not believe that they can "claim it if they name it," those who don't believe that God wants us all to be flying our private jets from place to place, may be the ones most negatively affected by this doctrine of devils. Because we don't believe in the health-and-wealth gospel, we may find it all too easy to not believe the promises of God.

MORE THAN THE LAST OLD TESTAMENT BOOK

While I can't speak for all believers, I can speak for myself. The Devil has certainly confused me on the book of Malachi. Here is one book of the Bible that I remember for all the wrong reasons. When the book comes to mind, I am more apt to consider where it comes in the Bible than I am to actually consider its message. I come to the book as if it were some kind of cliffhanger television episode, wondering what God had to say before creating four hundred years of prophetic silence. The second thing that comes to my mind may be even worse. I remember that tired old joke: Who was the first Italian prophet in the Bible? The answer is Malachi, only here we pronounce it "Malachee." In neither case do I think through the actual content of the book.

A case could be made that the book of Malachi was written to a group of

bitter people who were disappointed in the promises of God. The promises
themselves were grand enough. The people certainly seemed to believe those
promises. But Malachi was sent to explain to God's people why God apparently didn't keep His end of the bargain.

During the time of the exile, through many of the prophets, God promised that when the children of Israel returned, their kingdom would be more
glorious than it ever had been. They were told that Judah would be more
potent, more rich than at any time in her history. Her temple would be a
marvel of the world. In time, the people of God returned from exile. They
rebuilt Jerusalem. They rebuilt the walls. They rebuilt the temple. They did
as God had called them to do. But the promised blessings did not come.
Judah was still under a foreign power. Prosperity eluded her. The temple
wasn't a wonder of the world. In fact, it wasn't even on par with its former
glory. So God sent the prophet Malachi to tell His people why this was. The
book of Malachi is a textbook case against the errors of the health-and-wealth
teachers, for it reminds us with potent clarity that God is not some sort of
celestial vending machine, wherein we input this or that and out comes all
that we wish for.

Malachi begins his prophetic message by reminding Judah that God does
indeed love her:

> "I have loved you," says the LORD. But you say, "How have you
> loved us?" "Is not Esau Jacob's brother?" declares the LORD.
> "Yet I have loved Jacob but Esau I have hated. I have laid waste
> his hill country and left his heritage to jackals of the desert."
> (1:2–3)

After this encouraging beginning, however, Malachi goes on to cata-
log the sins of the people. First, he chastens the priests for offering polluted
sacrifices:

"A son honors his father, and a servant his master. If then I am
a father, where is my honor? And if I am a master, where is
my fear? says the LORD of hosts to you, O priests, who despise
my name. But you say, 'How have we despised your name?'
By offering polluted food upon my altar. But you say, 'How
have we polluted you?' By saying that the LORD's table may be
despised. When you offer blind animals in sacrifice, is that not
evil? And when you offer those that are lame or sick, is that not
evil? Present that to your governor; will he accept you or show
you favor? says the LORD of hosts." (1:6–8)

The people are rebuked because their worship has become routine to
them. (Here, too, the Devil is efficient. He has persuaded "high church"
opponents that liturgy is mere ritualism, and on the other hand he has persuaded "high church" proponents that liturgy can never reduce down to
ritualism. Once again, he has us coming and going.) They go through the
right motions, but their hearts, God suggests, are far from Him.

Next, God speaks to Judah about the issue of divorce:

And this second thing you do. You cover the LORD's altar with
tears, with weeping and groaning because he no longer regards
the offering or accepts it with favor from your hand. But you
say, "Why does he not?" Because the LORD was witness between
you and the wife of your youth, to whom you have been faith-
less, though she is your companion and your wife by covenant.
(2:13–14)

Eventually, Malachi gets to the most stunning rebuke of all. Before we
get to it, however, we might be wise to consider another great success of the
Serpent. He has persuaded much of the evangelical church of the foolish

notion that all sins are equally heinous. He has done this by twisting several points of Scripture. In James 2:10 we read, "For whoever keeps the whole law but fails in one point has become accountable for all of it." Jesus, as well, in the Sermon on the Mount taught that those who hate their brothers without cause have broken the sixth commandment and those who have lusted in their hearts have broken the seventh. From this, some have jumped to the conclusion that all sins are equally wicked, which does not follow. If we break a portion of the law, we have broken the law. If we hate unjustly, we have broken the commandment. But it simply does not follow that hatred is the same as first-degree murder or that failing to tithe on one's spice garden is the same as grand theft.

In chapter 3 of Malachi, we enter into this reality, that some sins are worse than others. We know, for instance, that it's a bad thing to steal. It's a bad (and dangerous) thing to steal from mobsters. It's a bad thing to steal from your employer. It's a bad thing to steal from little old ladies. It's a bad thing to steal candy from babies. I don't believe, however, that it can get any worse than stealing from God. This is Malachi's charge:

> "Will man rob God? Yet you are robbing me. But you say, 'How have we robbed you?' In your tithes and contributions. You are cursed with a curse, for you are robbing me, the whole nation of you." (3:8–9)

I'm fairly confident that when God's people raised their complaint, wondering why God wasn't blessing them like He'd promised, they weren't expecting such serious charges.

Once more, through the diabolical ministrations of the Serpent, we come to texts like these and see them not as occasions for repentance but as an occasions for theological debate. We sit down together to try to figure out whether tithing is only an Old Testament thing or applies in our day as well. We wonder whether our tithes should be figured on our net or gross. We debate whether the whole tithe must go to our local churches or whether we are allowed to give some to parachurch ministries. We bicker over these points so long that we lose sight of the shock of this text: men—and not just those living in Judah, circa 400 BC—rob God. God is telling us why He will not bless us, why we His people are insignificant, and our response is to have an argument amongst ourselves about technicalities.

FACE TO FACE WITH SHOCKING GRACE

As much as I might like to explore the potency of this prophecy, however, that is not my goal in this chapter or in this book. We do have a great problem believing God when He gives us His law. But this book is supposed to teach us to better believe His grace. The point here isn't merely to escape the clutches of the prosperity gospel, though that would be a good thing. The point isn't merely to learn to pay our tithes, though that would be a good thing, too. The point is to be brought face to face with the shocking grace of God. God tells the children of Judah, and us:

> "Bring the full tithe into the storehouse, that there may be food
> in my house. And thereby put me to the test, says the LORD of
> hosts, if I will not open the windows of heaven for you and pour
> down for you a blessing until there is no more need." (3:10)

Malachi begins by telling the children of Judah why God has not been blessing them. He catalogs their many sins against the living God, coming to a climax by reminding them that they are robbing God. The next thing from the prophet is this incredible promise. "Bring the tithes in," God says, "and see if I don't bury you in blessing." We respond by giving this promise the Bronx cheer. Because this text is a favorite proof text of the health-and-wealth crowd, we determine it must not be any good, forgetting, of course, that it is the very Word of God. When the Devil quoted Scripture back at Jesus during the temptation in the wilderness, saying, "If you are the Son of God, throw yourself down, for it is written, 'He will command his angels concerning you,' and, 'On their hands they will bear you up, lest you strike your foot against a stone'" (Matt. 4:6), Jesus didn't respond by suggesting that what the Devil quoted was no good or could not possibly be true. Neither should we do so.

It is certainly possible that our refusal to believe this promise isn't driven by distaste for those who abuse this promise. It may very well be that our unbelief is born, once again, out of the sheer prodigality of the promise. It seems, like many of the promises we have already looked at, too good to be true. Doesn't this text seem to suggest that if we pay our tithes, God will bless us in a mighty way? Doesn't it sound like it is saying, in fact, that if we will be faithful in giving God our tithes, He will open the very storehouse of heaven on us? It seems as if it is saying these things for this simple reason—it *is* saying these things. This is the plain meaning of the text, and we are in trouble when we try to get at that meaning by beginning with what the text doesn't mean.

So let's begin with what it does mean. God says to Judah, and to us as well, that we ought to test Him, that we ought to see what will happen when we pay our tithes. What will happen, God tells us, is that He will shower us with blessing. I know we're itching to get out from under this promise, but there it is. God said it, and He meant it.

Of course, there are appropriate caveats. The health-and-wealth hucksters, after all, have abused the text. First, this promise does not mean that we can treat God like a celestial slot machine. All that has preceded this promise in Malachi is background for the promise. You cannot simply pay your tithe and expect necessarily to receive the blessing of God. If you pay your tithe but give inappropriate sacrifices, God will not bless. If you pay your tithe but your heart is far from Him, He will not bless. If you pay your tithe and trade in your wife for a newer model, He will not bless.

Second, this promise, like many of the promises of God, is a proverbial promise rather than a contractual one. That is, God is telling us His pattern of behavior. God is not promising that we will reap a return of X percent or above if we pay our tithes. Our own proverbs operate in the same way. No one would want to argue against the notion that a stitch in time generally saves nine. Neither would anyone doubt that perhaps sometimes a stitch in time might only save eight, and on rare occasions could cause you to miss your deadline. If, for instance, one were given to financial folly, such that a windfall would do more harm than good, God probably would not send such a windfall.

Third, this promise can be fulfilled in any number of ways that are less crass than the slot-machine model. God's promise, for instance, may come about more corporately than individually. That is, it may be that when a nation faithfully tithes, that nation can expect God to pour out financial blessing on it. God gives the promise, after all, in a corporate context in Malachi. He is not merely talking to individuals who have failed to pay their tithes. He is talking to Judah as a whole. It may be that the blessing will come to the church broadly speaking or to those local churches that faithfully tithe.

BLESSED WITH A MORE GRATEFUL HEART

There is an even more important way in which this promise might be fulfilled. The blessing might not end up being a fatter bank account. The blessing might come in the form of a more grateful heart. It should not surprise us that in these United States we tend to have a rather distorted view of what it means to be poor. Most of those we consider poor in the Western world are better off than most of the people who have ever lived on the planet. In America, poverty, generally speaking, doesn't mean being in danger of starvation. Instead, it mean having a car that is old and run down, or a home that is shabby. What we call poverty isn't really poverty, but the pain that exists because of the gap between what we believe is our due and what God has provided. We feel poor because we think we should be living a lifestyle beyond that which we are living.

What if, when we pay our tithe, God blesses us not by moving us up the economic ladder a step or two, but by giving us thankful hearts for what we already have been given? What if He drives far from us the folly of a spirit of entitlement and causes us to rejoice in the blessings He already has showered on us? Isn't it strange, and a sure sign that we still suffer from this spirit of entitlement, that this kind of a blessing seems somehow lesser to us than greater wealth?

When we pay our tithes, we are already on our way to wealth that is the blessing of a thankful heart. When we give back to God ten percent of what He has given us, are we not affirming to God (at least when we do this in the way God calls us to do it, cheerfully) that we can get along just fine with less than what He has given us? Are we not affirming to Him, and to ourselves, that we are blessed well beyond what we deserve?

Once again, however, God is not a vending machine. He will not bless us if we give fifty percent of what He has given us but our hearts are far from Him and we fail to honor Him. One of the most important ways to honor Him, however, is to believe His promises. God virtually throws down the gauntlet here, taunting the children of Israel. "Go ahead," He says, "try Me. If you do this one thing, you won't know what hit you." If we fail to believe Him, we are slapping His face with that same gauntlet.

While the Serpent may be efficient, God is far more efficient. He is not only making a great promise here in Malachi, He is also teaching us a great deal about the nature of wealth. First, He is telling us that wealth can be a good thing. God does not treat material prosperity as some kind of icky thing that we ought to try to avoid. If God calls prosperity a blessing, we ought to believe Him. At the same time, by tying this message to the tithe, He is reminding us that there are far more important things than simply accumulating wealth. To live *in* prosperity can be a great and divine blessing. To live *for* this blessing is the way of death. As we return a token of what He has given to us, we remember both of these truths.

In the church where I serve, we take up the tithes and offerings. Some churches, perhaps trying to avoid offending their visitors, do not do this. We also reject the view that the giving of tithes and offerings marks a time-out for a "word-from-our-sponsor moment" in the service. We see it instead as an act of worship. As the tithes and offerings are brought forward, all the congregation stands. We affirm in so doing not that God owns ten percent, but that God owns all that we have and all that we are. We have been bought with a price. We belong to Him. We pray each Lord's Day that in giving these tithes and offerings we would remember that every good gift comes from His hand, that we would remember that we belong to Him, and that He would be pleased to send us the blessing of allowing us to make known the glory of the reign of His Son.

As we take hold of this promise, we come to learn where our blessing comes from. We learn to discern as well where our cursing comes from. But what may be the greatest blessing of all is this: we learn that God is the one who is sovereign over all these things. God, not your mean-spirited boss, determines how much He will prosper you. God, not the exigencies of the marketplace, determines what kind of blessing He will give you. As we learn to believe this, as we learn to rest in His sovereignty over our pocketbooks, we are better able to put to death envy. We are better able to rejoice with those who rejoice. We are better able to give thanks for our daily bread.

Here is a promise wherein we are able to measure our belief. I suggest we try it out. Better still, God calls us to try it out. If we do, He will open the very storehouse of heaven.

CHAPTER EIGHT

MOUNTAINS CAST INTO THE SEA

MARK 11:22–24

I t has been known to happen that a local pastor calls me into town to be his hired gunslinger. The pastor knows that I happen to share a conviction with him that might not go down easily with his parishioners. I'm brought in to teach a conference or a seminar. My job is to lay the conviction before the congregation, to try to persuade them, to take any bile they might have against the conviction, and then to leave town. It doesn't happen often, but it does happen. Having been blessed with the spiritual gift of thick skin, it's a role I'm happy to play.

There is, however, in the end, a better way for me to be a help to the pastor of a local church. Whether or not I've been invited to speak in order to teach some hard truths, I have at least one goal of which the pastor isn't typically aware. I certainly want to encourage the saints. I want to be true to the Word. I want to be a good and gracious guest. That is, I realize I haven't been invited to undo those convictions the pastor and I don't share. However, my goals include helping the congregation better understand and appreciate their pastor. I come as a pastor, but not as the pastor of the people to whom I am speaking. I have a perspective they might miss. That is why I try, wherever I am and whatever I have been asked to speak about, to help my hearers understand that it is not an easy thing to be a pastor.

Those in the pastorate face any number of hardships. Pastors are often, though not always, underpaid. While that would be a great thing to try to fix, it is not the hardest thing about being a pastor. Pastors are often, though not always, overworked. This, too, would be a great thing to try to fix, but it is not the hardest thing about being a pastor. Pastors are often, though not always, treated with very little respect. One poll ranked clergy as slightly more honorable and trustworthy than lawyers, and slightly less honorable and trustworthy than used-car salesmen. This, too, would be a great thing to fix, but it is not the hardest thing about being a pastor. The hardest thing about being a pastor, I explain when I speak, is the grievous pain he goes through as he watches the sheep whom he loves self-destruct. Nothing is more difficult for a shepherd than watching sheep batter their heads against a wall until their wool is bloody.

On the other hand, a congregation can best encourage its pastor not by giving him a nice raise or by zealously guarding his time and his reputation. Those steps may be perfectly fitting. But the pastor's greater joy, his greater encouragement, flows from seeing his sheep thriving, growing in grace, and bearing much of the fruit of the Spirit.

This is true not only of pastors, but others as well. While I may not be a pastor to you, that is nonetheless my desire in writing this book. I want to see the people of God grow in grace and wisdom. I want to see God's people better reflect the image of the one who bought them. I am writing this book in faith, on faith, asking that God might make us more a people of faith.

It is faith, and faith alone, that secures for us the finished work of Christ.

One could argue, indeed I *would* argue, that of all the things the church has lost or obscured over the years, no greater recovery was ever made than that which God brought us through the life and work of Martin Luther, the recovery of the doctrine of justification by faith alone. I pray the church never again will lose sight of this truth, that we always will remember that adding to our faith is a failure of faith, and worse, another gospel. Luther likewise recovered for us the doctrine of *sola Scriptura*, Scripture alone. He affirmed rightly that Scripture alone provides absolute truth, that it alone has the words of eternal life.

While we rejoice over these grand recoveries, however, we need to be on our guard. The victory for the church that came through the Reformation was not the end of the battle between the Seed of the woman and the seed of the Serpent. The Devil does not leave us alone once we embrace the *solas* of the Reformation. When we recover any biblical truth, we can be assured of two things. First, the Devil will not give up. Second, he will try a different strategy. One strategy he has taken with respect to *sola Scriptura* has been to encourage us to believe in and defend the doctrine while not looking to Scripture. Believing in the Bible and believing the Bible are not synonymous.

TWISTING THE TRUTH ABOUT FAITH

In like manner, the Devil has taken the very faith we have recovered and made hay where he could. One of his successes, in light of the Reformation, is rather ironic. He has encouraged us to denigrate the role, scope, and purpose of faith itself. He has encouraged us to see faith, though few of us would make this claim consciously, as something we exercise at one time or in one direction. We sometimes seem to think we exercise faith at the moment of salvation but move on from there without it. Or we exercise faith, trusting in the finished work of Christ, and go on trusting in that finished work of Christ. But outside of salvation, faith has little importance to us. It is true enough that we must trust in the finished work of Christ, and do so not just once but always. Indeed, all who trust fully in Christ alone will so trust always. But Jesus commanded the disciples to teach people to observe all the things that He had commanded (Matt. 28:20). We are to believe all that He says, even as we are to do all that He commands.

Is it not true that this is of the very essence of what it means to be a disciple of Christ? Is not spiritual growth the same thing as growing in our capacity for faith, our capacity to believe God? It is my all-too-common prayer that God would bless me, would sanctify me. I ask Him to help me, of little faith, to believe Him. I cry out to Him like the man with the demon-possessed son, "I believe; help my unbelief!" (Mark 9:24b). As we believe Him more and more, we are made more into His image, and His glory is made all the more manifest.

Jesus Himself makes much the same point, calling us to believe God. His goal here is more about our believing and less about the moving of mountains. The trouble is, once again, Jesus ends up sounding like a faith healer: "Have faith in God. Truly, I say to you, whoever says to this mountain, 'Be taken up and thrown into the sea,' and does not doubt in his heart, but believes that what he says will come to pass, it will be done for him. Therefore I tell you, whatever you ask in prayer, believe that you have received it, and it will be yours" (Mark 11:22–24).

Does it not sound as if Jesus is saying that there is a relationship between our faith and the effectiveness of our prayers? Here He not only feeds the notion, so popular among faith healers, that we need only "name it" in order to claim it, but provides us with an out when things don't go as we would hope. If the thing we pray for, whether it be health, wealth, or some other thing, does not come our way in the end, we can write it off as a failure of belief on our part. This diabolical line of reasoning is not merely hypothetical. I have close friends who have suffered from terrible maladies. Seeking relief, they turned to those who embrace this kind of theology. They were told, "You must believe even now that you have already been healed." When the promised healing did not come through, things were made worse when my friends were told, "You haven't been healed because you did not have enough faith." Now they suffer not only from bodies ravaged by sin but souls mauled by this foolishness.

It is often the case, however, that we take out our frustration over the misuse of a particular text of the Bible on the text itself rather than the misuse. We write off the verse, satisfying ourselves with the fact that we know what it doesn't mean, when we ought to be seeking to find out what it does mean, that we might believe it. We too often fall off the other side of the horse. Jesus here is not turning God into a cosmic vending machine that takes its coinage in faith. However, He is making an incredibly powerful promise, one we don't want to miss out on.

CURSING THE FRUITLESS FIG TREE

To better understand the scope of the promise, we would be wise to consider the context in which it is given. It comes in the context of Passion Week. Jesus has enjoyed His triumphal entry into Jerusalem. On the next day, however, as He is heading out of Bethany, Jesus, being hungry, sees a fig tree with leaves. However, it is not, the text tells us, the season for figs, so the tree has no fruit. Jesus declares, "May no one ever eat fruit from you again" (Mark 11:14). Later that day, Jesus dramatically cleanses the temple, preaching that it is to be a house of prayer, but that those in power have made it a den of thieves. The very next day, Peter finds the fig tree withered and brings it to the attention of Jesus. Then Jesus makes His claim about praying with belief.

By this point in His earthly ministry, Jesus has performed countless miracles. The disciples have seen the blind regain their sight and the lame walk. Demons have been cast out and water has been turned into wine. Every one of these miracles, please note, has been positive. Jesus brings life, health, and freedom. Here, however, He brings destruction on a simple fig tree. The lips that heretofore had pronounced blessing are now announcing curses. This is less a hard saying of Jesus and more a hard doing. Gentle Jesus, meek and mild, has left the scene. Now we witness the whip-bearing, tree-cursing Jesus.

We would be wise to remember that at all times Jesus is the Judge of the world. Here He pronounces judgment, as is His calling. The specific judgment is against the hypocrisy of the Pharisees. Just as the fig tree has the look of life, in having leaves, but has no fruit, so the Pharisees have a form of godliness but not its power. Thus, the tree is condemned and shown to have been powerless from the start. Suddenly, Jesus starts talking about faith and the moving of mountains.

Years ago, I had the opportunity to tour the Holy Land. Our guide, James Martin, was an expert in helping his students to see the significance of understanding the local geography and customs in order to grasp the meaning of Scripture. He was a veritable font of fascinating information, and so I was patient with him one day when his wisdom seemed to come forth with neither rhyme nor reason.

Our group was just outside Jerusalem, walking up a steep hill. We were planning to stop along the way at the traditional site of the resurrection of Lazarus. Jim, however, was talking to us about the Roman occupation and the Jewish tradition. He explained how difficult it was for pious Jews to live under Roman occupation. The rabbis constructed a lengthy tradition to provide wisdom in that difficult context. What, for instance, ought a pious man to do were he to come upon a small idol in the gutter while walking through the streets of Jerusalem? The Romans had myriad gods, and they weren't at all shy about making representations of them. Jim explained that the Jews were told to pick up such a found idol, to take it to the nearest body of water, and to throw it in. This symbolized their understanding that idols were demonic in origin and one day would be cast into the lake of fire.

Isn't that a nice little tidbit of information? Having finished with that story, we were instructed to turn around and to gaze out at the great open plain. We saw there two great hills or small mountains. The shorter of the two was flat on top, the taller more round. Jim explained that Herod the Great had ordered the top of the one hill to be removed and placed on the other. There, on top of the now taller hill, Herod built his winter palace. Once again, nice information, if a little disjointed. Then Jim tied these pieces together. He explained that it was his belief that it was at this spot that Jesus spoke these words from Mark 11. It was his conviction that Jesus said, pointing to the mountain that already had been moved once, the mountain that represented all the imperial power of Rome, "Whoever says to *this* mountain, 'Be taken up and thrown into the sea,' and does not doubt in his heart, but believes that what he says will come to pass, it will be done for him" (v. 23, emphasis added). He explained that he believed that Jesus was saying that Herod, and Rome with him, was demonic and would be overthrown one day.

My friend Jim may well have been right. Events like this help us understand the correct answer to what too often puzzles evangelicals. Why, we wonder, did the first-century disciples of Jesus constantly see Him as some sort of political revolutionary? I'd suggest it was because Jesus was, and is, some sort of political revolutionary. Jesus came to bring His kingdom, that kingdom that will swallow all others, that will have no end, and that has no borders. Read through Psalm 2 and see whether you can still maintain that the reign of Jesus is strictly a spiritual reality. Remember His promise to the disciples, just before He ascended to His throne, that all authority in heaven and on earth had been given to Him (Matt. 28:18).

While I am perfectly comfortable accepting this context for Jesus' promise here, I can't help but wonder whether what He said wasn't even more radical. There is another mountain in the context, the movement of which would be even more astonishing. Isn't it at least possible that Jesus isn't speaking of Herod's palace but the very temple of God? Jesus has already cleansed the temple, bringing judgment against it and against those who are in charge. He has already pronounced judgment against the hypocrisy of the Pharisees. When He speaks these words, He has been to the temple and is headed back toward the temple. Is He saying that the powers that be in the context of the temple are, like the Roman empire, demonic and idolatrous?

If this is the case, that our faith will topple not just voracious governments but false religions, the power of the promise is increased rather than diminished. A wicked religion is far more wicked than a wicked government. The latter can only oppress for a time. The former leads souls to an eternal hell. In either case, or rather in both cases, we see a connection between our faith and the very power to change the world.

STEPPING MORE DEEPLY INTO THE FAITH

Just as the abuse of this text by sundry faith healers should not cause us to miss the power of this promise, so these speculations about where Jesus may have been when making this promise, or to what He may have been referring, should not cause us to miss the broader point. The first step is for us to step more deeply into our faith. We must be more bold, more faithful, in believing God. The power wrought by such faith is not the relatively petty power it might take to prosper us further. It is not the relatively anemic power it would take to grant us health and long life. Rather, our faith has the power to change history, to tear down strongholds, to make known the reign of Christ over all things.

As we considered in chapter 6, the way whereby we might see the great power of God at work in our prayers is to begin to pray for those truly great things God has promised. As our desires begin to intersect with the very promises of God, we will see our prayers answered in great power. Consider, for instance, both the power of the Pharisees, as represented by the temple, and the power of Rome itself.

Less than forty years after Jesus made His startling promise, the temple was figuratively "thrown into the sea." In AD 70, the Roman army laid siege to Jerusalem. The entire city was razed to the ground, and the temple was left without one stone upon another. The Christians, however, survived this holocaust. When the army descended on Jerusalem, those outside the kingdom fled *for* the city, while those within the church fled *from* the city. They scattered, taking the good news of the kingdom of Jesus Christ with them across the known world.

As they went, more and more men, women, and children were brought into the kingdom. Soon the Christian faith grew so strong that Rome scrapped its policy of tolerance and began to persecute the Christians. By the tens of thousands they were put to death. Nero was known to cover living Christians with tar, tie them down, and light them so that his garden parties would be well-lit. The Appian Way was lined with mile after mile of Christians crucified for their faith. Countless more went to their deaths as a form of entertainment in the coliseums of the empire. There we witnessed the power of faith, as the blood of the martyrs became the seed of the church. Eventually, Constantine, early in the fourth century, signed the Edict of Milan, declaring the Roman empire to be Christian. His successor, Julian the Apostate, sought to undo the work of Constantine, but knew that he failed. As he lay on his deathbed, he is said to have declared, "Thou hast conquered, oh pale Galilean."

Our calling is to recognize that faith matters, that as we believe all that God has told us, God will make known the glory of His power. We are told these things, given these promises, that we might grow in grace and wisdom. As time marches on, as the kingdom of God advances, we will find ourselves facing our own principalities and powers. We will find ourselves up against long odds. It is then we will be called to remember this promise and to remember our call to faith.

Imagine if you had been Martin Luther, one lonely monk facing all the power of Roman Catholicism. Would you have had the faith to pray that God would move mountains? Clyde Manschreck, who served as the editor of the second volume of *A History of Christianity* (Baker Books, 1984), records for us how Luther prayed the evening before he would make his final appearance before the Diet of Worms:

"O almighty and everlasting God! How terrible is this world! Behold it openeth its mouth to swallow me up, and I have so little trust in Thee! How weak is the flesh and how powerful is Satan! If it is in the strength of this world only that I must put my trust, all is over! My last hour is come, my condemnation has been pronounced. O God! O God! O God! Do Thou help me against all the wisdom of the world! Do this; Thou shouldst do this; Thou alone, for this is not my work but Thine! I have nothing to do here, nothing to contend for with these great ones of the world! I should desire to see my days flow on peaceful and happy. But the cause is Thine, and it is a righteous and eternal cause, O Lord! Help me! Faithful and unchangeable God! In no man do I put my trust. It would be vain—all that is of man is uncertain, all that cometh of man fails. O God! My God, hearest Thou me not? My God, art Thou dead? No! No, Thou canst not die! Thou hidest Thyself only! Thou hast chosen me for this work. I know it well! Act then, O God, stand at my side, for the sake of Thy well-beloved Son, Jesus Christ, who is my defense, my shield and my strong tower.

Lord, where stayest Thou? O my God, where art Thou? Come, come! I am ready to lay down my life for Thy truth, patient as a lamb. For the cause of justice—it is Thine! O I will never separate myself from Thee, neither now nor through eternity! And though the world may be filled with devils, though my body, which is still the work of Thy hands, should be slain, be stretched upon the pavement, be cut in pieces, reduced to ashes—my soul is Thine! Yes, I have the assurance of Thy word. My soul belongs to Thee! It shall abide forever with Thee. Amen. O God! Help me! Amen."

Luther was a man who believed God, who rested in His power. And the power of that resting, by God's grace, moved mountains. All the world was changed and the gospel was recovered. Our calling is to walk by faith, to believe God's promises, even when all seems to be against us. As we do so, we too will find ourselves used of God to change the world. If we will believe, God will move mountains.

CHAPTER NINE

ALL THINGS WORK TOGETHER

ROMANS 8:28

This morning began with a brisk three-mile walk. The weather was perfect, and walking beside me was my dear wife. We enjoyed our exercise and our conversation. As we started to ascend our driveway, our beloved dog raced down to greet us. Once in the house, I quickly cleaned myself off and headed into town with my youngest daughter for step one of her sixth birthday celebration. In town, we enjoyed breakfast together at her favorite fast-food joint. While I am not a fan of this particular fast-food joint, or any other, it does serve a breakfast sandwich of which I am rather fond. There I sat with my cute-as-a-button little girl, savoring a meal that undid the benefits of my walk. Now here I sit in my office, hard at work on my book. It's been a good morning.

Not all mornings go like this. Sometimes the dog has gotten into the trash and made a horrible mess. Sometimes my children are not celebrating

birthdays but are testing my nerves. Some mornings I don't have the opportunity to exercise with my wife because one of us is sick. Sometimes I'm just
lazy. Sometimes our days begin not with peace but with stress.

I was musing not long ago about my habits in dealing with stress. Less
than six weeks ago, I was teaching in Myanmar, formerly known as Burma,
a troubled country in Southeast Asia. Myanmar is predominately Buddhist.
The government is a military dictatorship that at present rules under martial
law. I was given the opportunity to teach a group of young pastors and elders
there, men who were zealous for the faith. I had been looking forward to the
trip, but I had a large handful of fears to deal with. The process of securing a
visa was not simple and crystal clear. Mine came in the mail two days before
my scheduled departure. My flights would take more than forty hours in
both directions. I would be travelling through two countries where I did not
know the language to get to yet another country where I did not know the
language.

I realized I had gone through something of a cycle about this trip. When
the opportunity first came up, I was terribly excited. As the trip grew closer,
my anxiety grew. I spent a few weeks struggling with sleep. When the time
came to leave, however, I suppressed my fears and went on my way. Once I
was safely through customs at my final destination, I went through a period
of wonder as I enjoyed the blessing of visiting a strange land. As our taxi
traversed the distance between the airport and the hotel, I hung my head out
the window like a dog as I took it all in. My fears diminished still more as I
got to know my hosts in the country. Finally, I was at ease.

STRESS-BUSTING LITURGIES

I suspect most of us have internal liturgies we go through when confronted
with challenges. Often when I'm confronted with circumstances that cause
me to lose my peace, I go through a two-part liturgy followed by a three-part

liturgy. I begin by asking myself this question: What's the worst that could happen? Part two of that first liturgy is to remember that whatever the worst is, it's not that bad. There's nothing like a little careful, dispassionate thought to help quell fears.

The second process involves three very simple questions. It is important to answer the questions with the utmost objectivity, to fight the temptation to twist and distort. The first question I ask when I find myself battling against stress is this: What am I due? It is all too easy for us to lose sight of what we are. We move through this world forgetting that we are, in ourselves, an unhappy joining together of dust and rebellion. Because of our rebellion, we look at the world and its Maker as if we are owed peace and comfort. The truth of the matter is that no matter what kind of hardship we might find ourselves going through, every human on the planet, even those who are outside God's electing grace, moves through his days in a context of unfathomable grace.

Theologians, who make distinctions for a living, wisely distinguish between what they call God's common grace and His special grace. God, they affirm, showers those whom He has chosen with a particular grace, blessing them with new hearts, giving them the gift of faith, and covering their sins with the blood of Christ. But even those outside the kingdom receive sundry kindnesses from their Maker. God, after all, sends the rain on the just and the unjust. This grace is rightly called "common" if we understand the word to refer not to the quality of the grace but to its extent. Everyone receives this grace, but it too is altogether amazing. We are all rebels against the God who made us, who sustains us, who showers us with this grace. What we are due is eternal torment. This is what God owes us, according to a strict standard of justice.

So before we even get to the next two questions, our fears ought to ease. We ought to realize immediately that whatever we are going through, it falls well short of what our rebellion is due. We all, Christians and non-Christians, move from grace to grace on this side of the veil. We all ought to be stunned by how well things are going for us, no matter how badly things may be going for us.

The second question moves us beyond merely asking what we are due and remembering in a vague way that we have it better than we ought. It asks us to consider what we actually have. The question is: What have I been given? Here we enter into the depth of the blessing God has given us. We enjoy much more than merely not getting what we deserve. We receive from Him our daily bread. We enjoy relationships with people we love. We are all richly blessed.

Before writing the paragraph just above, I was called away from my work. My office is in my home. Since we are raising seven children, it is not at all unusual for us to go through what I call "sitcom moments." These are events and circumstances that tend to show up as stock plot devices on television. This afternoon we had a re-run. For the third or fourth time we went through the "bubbles filling the room scene." It seems one of my young daughters used the soap for hand-washing dishes in the dishwasher. Now, I don't like having my work interrupted. And I don't like the tedious job of cleaning up all those bubbles. But as I went upstairs, there was my little girl who had done this. God could have kept my kitchen perfectly clean and dry. But instead He gave me this precious little girl. I don't deserve this bundle of love, who delights in nothing more than giving me hugs, writing me love notes, and trying to help clean up. Every evening, like the blessed man in Psalm 128, I sit at my supper table with my dear wife and all seven of our blessed olive plants. If I remember this in times of hardship, I remember that I have been given much.

The third question is the most difficult to answer objectively. It asks of me that I gaze into that which is too bright to see. I know, though I don't know well enough, what I am due. I know, though I don't know well enough, what I have been given. But what have I been promised? When I take my eyes off my troubles and look instead to God's promises, my troubles melt in a sea of joy. As we will consider later in this book, we will see Him as He is. We will be with Him. We will be like Him. We will enjoy at His right hand pleasures forevermore. This is not something we merely hope for. This is the very promise of the sovereign God. How can we despair when He who made all things, whose word is truth, promises us that our joy will be such that no eye has seen it, no ear has heard it, and it has not entered our minds to think it. However objectively we seek to answer this question, God promises we will come short.

This question, however, as potent as it may be in helping me get over my fears and troubles, yet has a weakness. In sending us hardships, God does not call us merely to hold our breath, knowing that a better day is coming. Our calling isn't to suffer through our threescore and ten, knowing that things will get better in the end and make all our suffering worthwhile. We do not manage this hardship or that by means of a promise about the future promise. We do so in light of a present promise, a present reality. The good news isn't that we can endure a present hardship because of future blessing. The good news is that the hardship itself is, according to this biblical promise, the blessing.

A CLEARER VIEW OF PROVIDENCE

Thus, this promise helps us rid ourselves of what I call the "Superman theory of providence." According to this theory, we see God as acting in space and time, but only when danger rears its ugly head. We narrowly escape an ugly car accident and we thank God for preserving us—as if God were sitting in heaven and noticed the two cars coming together, so He jumped into His celestial phone booth and flew down to earth to keep the cars from colliding. To be sure, God does sometimes protect us from car accidents. But they are near accidents that this same providence brought to pass. He is as sovereign over the cars getting so close as He is over them not hitting. It's not that God sees the bad thing coming down the pike and figures out a way to bring some good out of it. Instead, the bad thing is the very means of the good thing.

Here is God's promise: "And we know that for those who love God all things work together for good, for those who are the called according to his purpose" (Rom. 8:28). This text is familiar to most of us. Sadly, that familiarity too often has bred contempt. Some would say that this promise, which ought to be a great comfort to us during times of trial, shouldn't be so used. To quote this text to a person in trouble seems to some to be trite and clichéd. Let me give a trite warning: We ought never to treat the Word of God in this way. This promise comes to us straight from the lips of God Himself, and it is our duty, and should be our delight, to believe it.

Most of us, when we look back over the course of our lives, see things we regret. One of my deepest regrets is my failure, especially in my youth, to redeem the time. I think about the books I could have read, the Scripture I could have memorized, and the spiritual disciplines I could have acquired. I am ashamed instead of the television shows I watched, the trivia I memorized, and the unhealthy habits I developed along the way. I regret my failure to improve on the blessings God gave me.

Not all of my regrets, however, are in the distant past. I have had failures as a pastor, times when I didn't care sufficiently well for sheep in my flock. I think of the wounds these sheep carry with them, in part because of my failures. I continue to fail to watch rightly over that flock closest to me, my family. All of this ought to lead me to repentance, which is a good thing, a needful thing. Most of us, because we don't really think about what we are due, do not repent well. Some of us, however, don't believe well either. That is, in light of our sin, our calling is to repent and believe, not repent and regret. Repentance is a blessing. Remorse is not.

Consider for a moment the scope of this promise. It covers even our sins. Paul does not tell us that some things work together. He does not tell us that most things work together. Instead, we are promised that *all* things work together for good. It is not just the hard providences God sends that work together for good. The promise even includes those times when we shoot ourselves in the foot.

We will better be able to believe this promise the better we are able to remember our goal, our end, our purpose. If we believe that we were put on this earth to acquire personal peace and affluence, we will have a difficult time believing that assaults on that peace and affluence are in fact good things. If, however, we understand that our goal is something separate from the goal of those outside the kingdom, that our end is something more significant than personal peace and affluence, then we can begin to see how these hardships might in fact be good things. The Westminster Shorter Catechism, that great seventeenth-century work written to instruct the young in the basics of the Christian faith, begins with this question: "What is the chief end of man?" It answers, "Man's chief end is to glorify God, and to enjoy him for ever." We exist that God's glory might be made manifest and that we might delight in Him always. This happens, in both instances, as we are made evermore like Him, as we grow in grace, as we are sanctified. This is where all things are moving, where every experience, good and bad, is taking us. This is the good that all things work together toward.

Everything, from my wife's diagnosis of cancer to the foaming bubbles all over my kitchen floor, works together for God's glory, for my wife's sanctification, and for my sanctification. This is why James tells us, "Count it all joy, my brothers, when you meet trials of various kinds, for you know that the testing of your faith produces steadfastness. And let steadfastness have its full effect, that you may be perfect and complete, lacking in nothing" (1:2–4). We're supposed to count our trials as joy because we are being sanctified through them and God is being glorified in them.

In principle, I trust, we don't have any objection to God making His glory known. We don't have any grand objection to our sanctification either. Our objection, more often than not, is with the means God chooses to bring these things to pass. We want these things, as long as they come to us easily and comfortably. We pray: "O Lord, please teach me humility. But don't humiliate me." Praise God that He does not take instruction from us. We would not accept such negotiations from our children. If they suggested that they were perfectly willing to be healthy, just so long as it didn't mean that they had to eat their vegetables and get to bed at a decent hour, we would not try to find a way to appease their desires. Neither does our Father in heaven do so when we behave in this way. Of course, were He so inclined, He could sanctify us immediately, without the use of means. He could send humility rays straight from heaven, were that in His interests. Instead, however, He has determined to tell the story of His glory by causing us to become more like His beloved Son in and through the hardships that He sends our way. We do not become like Him by wallowing in self-pity over these hardships, but by counting them all joy.

While God shows forth the glory of His grace to all mankind, this particular promise does carry one caveat. As we have noted, it is all things that work together for good, not merely some things. But it is not that all things work together for good to all people. This promise is restricted to a particular subset of humanity—to those who love God, who have been called according to His purpose. This is a promise given to you from God Himself, *if* you are in Christ. To doubt this promise is to doubt whether you are even in Christ. It is not that some Christians receive this promise while others do not. Whether God has called you to move through this life from happy moment to happy moment or whether He has called you to suffer in and for your faith, this promise is for you. All of us, then, ought to be rejoicing. We belong to Him; we are His clay. And He is about the business of molding us into works of eternal beauty.

Isn't it interesting what follows from this glorious promise? Romans 8:29–30 details for us what is sometimes called "the golden chain of salvation," or, for those who love Latin, the *ordo salutis*, theologian's language for the order of salvation. After we are told that all things work together for good for us, we are given a roadmap of that good: "For those whom he foreknew he also predestined to be conformed to the image of his Son, in order that he might be the firstborn among many brothers. And those whom he pre-destined he also called, and those whom he called he also justified, and those whom he justified he also glorified." The golden chain is introduced in His love and ends in glory.

FOREKNOWLEDGE IS
MORE THAN KNOWLEDGE

Please note something terribly important. When Paul speaks of God "fore-knowing" us, he does not merely mean to know beforehand. God, of course, knows all things before they come to pass. He is, after all, omniscient, all-knowing. He even "foreknows" those who are outside the kingdom, if we mean that He merely knows beforehand. What Paul is suggesting here is that God loves us beforehand, this "knowledge" meaning something far more significant than mere recognition. This knowledge is like unto that "knowledge" by which we are told in Genesis that Adam "knew" his wife and she conceived. Paul is speaking of God's love for His chosen in Christ from before all time.

In this all-powerful and eternal love, God has determined far more than that we would merely be good. His purpose, according to this text, is that we would be conformed to the image of His Son. We are not measuring up to some transcendent and abstract moral standard as we grow in grace and sanctification. Instead, we are growing more and more like Jesus Himself. Sanctification has become, I fear, at least in Calvinistic circles, more of a doctrine to be studied than a calling to be pursued. Of course it is a biblical doctrine, and so study of it is appropriate. But the first lesson we ought to learn is that it is our calling, the goal we are to pursue. For this reason, though it has yet to catch on, I much prefer the term "Jesus-ification" to sanctification. We are becoming more and more like Jesus.

In this reality, we see that God's dual purposes are truly in the end but one purpose. Because our sanctification is our Jesus-ification, our good and His glory end up being one and the same. His glory is shown forth in our sanctification. The glory of the Son, who is called "the express image of His person" (Heb. 1:3, NKJV), is to show forth the glory of the Father. Our glory is to show forth the glory of the Son. This is why we have been predestined by the Father. This is why we have been called by the Spirit. This is why we have been justified in the Son. It is all for glory, a glory that we share in Him.

We forget this all too often. Because we are still sinners, we set aside the glory of God's agenda and pursue the folly of our agenda. We do not wake up each morning determined to grow ever more like Jesus. Instead, we wake up determined to do this job or that, to win this contract, or to secure that raise. We wake up hoping our day will go "well," and we define such a day as one filled with comfort and ease. God, praise His name, is unconcerned about our foolish plans. Man, after all, proposes, but God disposes. He has a far greater agenda for us each day. He has determined to cause us to become more like His Son. He has determined that He will bring this to pass via sundry trials and challenges. When they hit us, because we are upside down and foolish, we wonder what has gone wrong with the world. We are confused because God has not cooperated with our agenda. Because we are fools, we think our plan wise and His actions foolish. We do not count it all joy but all frustration.

We must look at our circumstances and His promises objectively. If I were to ask you, "Would you rather have you plan your future or God plan your future?" or "Would you rather God pursued His agenda for you or your agenda for you?" which would you choose? We know God is wiser than we are. We know that God loves us far more than we love ourselves. We know that God knows the future and we do not. We know that all His desires are good and holy. Why, then, do we get so frustrated when the lawn mower won't start? Why do we so despair over the medical diagnosis? Whether it is a great burden or a small irritant, our frustration betrays that our hearts don't remember what our minds know.

We make this mistake, I believe, because of a prior mistake. Our goals are distorted in large part because we do not see the glory of the promise. That is, things such as comfort and ease, respect and prosperity, look more attractive to us precisely because our eyes refuse to see the glory of what has been promised to us. We do not count it all joy to be conformed to the image of the Son because we do not find the image of the Son something to be desired. We worry about who will be the next president or who our boss is at work precisely because we do not rejoice at the glory of the King of kings. The promise of God is that we are being made like Him, *Him*, the very King of Glory.

If, instead, we would delight in Him, if we would, by His grace, behold His glory more fully, if we would see through the veil more clearly, if we would draw near to Him in prayer and at His table, then we would know not where we are going but to whom. Then we would rejoice in every step of the journey. Then we would give thanks and would believe His promises. If we believed Him, we would wake each morning confident that the coming day, whatever it might bring, would bring us closer to being like Him. If we believed Him, we would go to sleep each evening without a care in the world. We would sleep soundly, because we would be sound enough to know that all that came to pass that day brought us closer to Him. We need not ask Him in our prayers to do us good all the days of our lives. He already has so promised. Instead, let us ask Him for this good, that He would help us to believe that He always does us good.

CHAPTER TEN

HE HAS OVERCOME THE WORLD

JOHN 16:33

There are at least two important reasons why we have such a difficult time believing the promises of God. The first and most glaring is our sin. Since the fall of Adam, we have found ourselves in a position where sin comes naturally to us, where our default position is to not believe God. It all began when Adam and Eve failed to believe God. Like them, we, their children, believe our father, the Father of Lies. We are skeptical of what God says and prefer to be as God, constructing reality out of our internal fantasies. We are, in short, fools.

God, after all, is altogether more than merely honest. It's not as though there is a universe out there that God has carefully studied. It isn't that He has collected all the data there is to know. God does not know all things because He attained that knowledge; He knows all things because all that is is by the very word of His power. He speaks, and reality comes to pass.

101

He says, "Let there be light," and there is light. His Word is to reality what Midas' touch was to gold. God doesn't merely intersect with truth, but is truth, immutably so.

To be as God, as the Serpent first promised in the garden, we have to construct reality. The difference between God's construction and ours is that His is real while ours is false. We have determined in our postmodern world that there is no reality outside ourselves to which we all must submit. Instead, we can each create reality, where stealing may be wrong for me but may be just fine for you, where Mozart may be music to you but the sound of fingernails on chalkboards may be music to me. In short, we prefer to believe ourselves rather than God, to believe the Serpent rather than the Father. This is the very nature of that most primordial of battles, the battle between the Seed of the woman and the seed of the Serpent, as it is laid down for us in Genesis 3. The one compelling question all the days of our lives is this: Will we believe God or not?

That still leaves a second reason for our struggle to believe God. We also have trouble believing Him because we are given to believing our eyes. For us, seeing is believing. We are all from Missouri (the "Show Me State") at the end of the day. We have difficulty believing the promises of God, those covenants of grace that we have been looking at together, because it doesn't look as if they will come to pass. The Devil delights for us to see with our eyes rather than to see through faith, what Scripture calls the assurance of things hoped for, the conviction of things *not seen* (Heb. 11:1, emphasis added). Satan's goal is less about tempting us to fall into more flamboyant sins and more about encouraging us not to believe God.

We don't believe, at a most basic level, that we who are in Christ move through our lives at peace with God. As such, we struggle with all manner of fears and insecurities. To help counter this, at Saint Peter Presbyterian Church, the church that I was honored to plant and where I continue to serve, we move each Sunday through a thoughtful liturgy. During our entire service we are about the business of renewing covenant with God. The service is a kind of conversation between God and us. He speaks to us and we reply, saying amen to all that He tells us. We begin, like most churches, with a call to worship. This is not understood as the pastor or the elders calling the congregation to worship. Instead, we recognize that God Himself calls us. He calls us to appear before Him, almost like an inspection in the armed services. God, the great King and General, comes to inspect His troops. We respond by obeying, but also by noting that we are not obedient. That is, the next step in our worship is our corporate confession of sin. Here we do not busy ourselves chronicling the sins we as individuals have committed in the previous week. There may be a time and place for that. Our goal, instead, is to acknowledge our nature. We do not declare, "These are the sins I have done." Instead, we affirm to Him, "Here we are, sinners, all of us."

While the service ends each week with the glory of God's feeding us at His table, it is at the beginning of the service that we enter into the joy of the gospel. God's response to our confession is called either the Declaration of Absolution or the Assurance of Pardon. Here the pastor reads one of God's great promises regarding His forgiveness: that He has removed our sins as far from us as the east is from the west, that Christ suffered in our place, that we are indeed forgiven. From here on, our service of worship is a celebration of that truth.

What, though, would our week look like if we were able to move forward with confidence of this peace with God? How powerful would we be in the building of His kingdom if we were truly free from fear, knowing that we are His, that He loves us with an everlasting love? Our joy, our peace, our fruit would make us truly more than conquerors. We would walk into battle utterly unassailable, confident in God's love for us. However, we don't believe this simple gospel promise. We don't believe we are at peace with Him.

SATAN MAKES WAR ON OUR PEACE

The Serpent brings forth his evidence in this manner. He seeks to persuade us that God does not love us, that He has not forgiven us, by pointing to our pain and suffering. Using our struggle as his evidence, he encourages us to live in fear that God may not love us. Or he tries another tack. Sometimes the Serpent may be quite content for us to believe God loves us, as long as we understand the suffering we are going through as a sign that God is powerless. "Sure," the Devil tells us, "God loves you, boodles and bunches. The trouble is, there's not a thing He can do about this hardship you're going through. I'm sure He'd love to help if He could, but, you know, what can He do?"

This temptation is one of the reasons why it is so important for us to understand God's sovereignty over all things. We do not affirm and defend the truth that God is indeed almighty so that we can win arguments with our friends. We believe God is sovereign over all things, including our suffering, based on the plain teaching of the Bible. But in believing it, we are better able to face those hardships in a context of faith, while believing God. When we remain committed to these two truths, that God does in fact love us and that He is in fact almighty over all things, then we are forced to this sound conclusion—the hardships we are going through are because of His sovereign love for us. He sends the suffering precisely because He loves us and because He is sovereignly about the business of remaking us into the image of His Son.

Consider for a moment what Jesus went into just as He was about to enter into His passion. John 16 begins, "I have said all these things to you to keep you from falling away" (v. 1). What were these things that He had spoken? He had said:

> If the world hates you, know that it has hated me before it hated
> you. If you were of the world, the world would love you as its
> own; but because you are not of the world, but I chose you

out of the world, therefore the world hates you. Remember the word that I said to you: "A servant is not greater than his master." If they persecuted me, they will also persecute you. If they kept my word, they will also keep yours. But all these things they will do to you on account of my name, because they do not know him who sent me. If I had not come and spoken to them, they would not have been guilty of sin, but now they have no excuse for their sin. Whoever hates me hates my Father also. If I had not done among them the works that no one else did, they would not be guilty of sin, but now they have seen and hated both me and my Father. But the word that is written in their Law must be fulfilled: "They hated me without a cause." But when the Helper comes, whom I will send to you from the Father, the Spirit of truth, who proceeds from the Father, he will bear witness about me. And you also will bear witness, because you have been with me from the beginning. (15:18–27)

Here Jesus warns the disciples that persecution is coming. He gives them context for that persecution, reminding them that He has and will suffer the same, explaining that those who will do the persecuting stand guilty already because of all that He has revealed to them.

Then Jesus begins to explain something of the scope of this suffering. His warning isn't that the disciples will suffer merely some level of social ostracism. Rather, "They will put you out of the synagogues. Indeed, the hour is coming when whoever kills you will think he is offering service to God" (16:2). I suspect that our eyes are arrested by the motives of these persecutors. Jesus tells us they will do these things while thinking they are serving God. I suspect, on the other hand, that the disciples have a different perspective. They might not even hear Jesus describe their motives, being still stuck on the part about others killing them.

In the next verse, Jesus explains again that these people do not know the Father. This is important too. Remember that the disciples have grown up within first-century Judaism. They have been taught to see those in authority there to be sitting in the seat of Moses. They are going to be tempted to conclude, knowing that they are sinners, that they are actually due the persecution they receive. Jesus reminds them they will be persecuted precisely because of the unbelief of the persecutors.

Next, Jesus further explains His reasons for explaining this, and explaining it now. He wants the disciples to know these things because they will need to remember them when the suffering comes. He is telling them now because He will not be with them when this persecution arises. Then follows a rather lengthy discussion of the meaning of these words. Jesus is speaking of two soon departures and one soon return. That is, He will be away from them from His arrest to His resurrection. Then, forty days later, He will ascend to the right hand of the Father.

Finally, the disciples think they have understood what Jesus has been saying: "Ah, now you are speaking plainly and not using figurative speech! Now we know that you know all things and do not need anyone to question you; this is why we believe that you came from God" (vv. 29–30). Jesus, in turn, warns them again, not at all persuaded that they understand what is coming upon them: "Do you now believe? Behold the hour is coming, indeed it has come, when you will be scattered, each to his own home, and will leave me alone. Yet I am not alone, for the Father is with me" (vv. 31–32).

This, Jesus reminds them, is God's plan. This suffering should not surprise them, not only because it makes sense (that is, that the disciples should suffer even as the Master does) but because it is God bringing this to pass—it is His plan. All of this hardship is exactly as it should be, He warns them. And so, in turn, He warns us.

WRONGLY ENVYING THE EYEWITNESSES

If you're like me, you have been tempted to jealousy sometimes in reading the Bible. Wouldn't it have been something, I wonder, to have witnessed the splitting of the Red Sea? Would it not have been delightful to watch Lazarus walk out of the tomb? While such envy is understandable, it loses sight of at least one profound blessing that we enjoy. We are reading all these stories already mindful of the resurrection of Jesus. The disciples, who witnessed countless miracles, had not yet seen Jesus walking alive out of His grave. I like to think if I had witnessed all Jesus' miracles that I would be a spiritual giant, that my faith would never waver. The trouble is, even we who live on this side of the resurrection, who know that Jesus is alive, lack faith. We don't believe God. Thus, we don't believe the shocking promise that Jesus then delivers any more than the disciples did: "I have said these things to you, that in me you may have peace. In the world you will have tribulation. But take heart, I have overcome the world" (v. 33).

Years ago, I served full-time on the staff of Ligonier Ministries, my father's well-known teaching work. Among my many functions at that time was to serve as a sort of gatekeeper for my father. Getting his ear could do great things for a person, a ministry, a movement. Some folks were insightful enough to realize that my time was a little less valuable than my father's, but that getting to me might be a path to getting to him. That was why I found two gentlemen in my office one day.

These young men embraced a heresy sometimes called Hymeneanism, sometimes called full preterism, sometimes called pantelism. These folks believe that all prophecy in the Bible already has come to pass. Now there are those, and I am one of them, who believe that many biblically prophesied events that others think are still in the future are actually in the past. We call ourselves partial preterists. The difference may seem small enough, but that small difference hinges on a central belief of the Christian faith from the beginning. Partial preterists still look forward to the final coming of Christ and to the resurrection of the dead. Full preterists expect no future bodily resurrection. Of course, the closer these folks could ally themselves with my father, the better things would go for them.

We sat down to visit and spent the first little while talking about areas of agreement. We considered together some of the more extreme views within the evangelical camp on the end times. We had pleasant debates over this text in Scripture and that. I was trying to help these gentlemen, and they thought they were trying to help me. It was all polite and collegial. And then I gave them this objection: there are still tears. If all prophecy has been fulfilled, then there is no better world to which we can look forward. I explained to these men that whatever arguments they might have in favor of their heresy, the world we live in underdelivers. If this world represents the fullness of the kingdom, then Jesus must have lost.

One does not have to embrace the heresy of full preterism in order to feel the weight of this objection. Jesus declares here that He already has overcome the world. We live in a world that is already under the full rule and reign of Jesus Christ. So why is there sickness, sin, and death? Why are we still suffering so, given this promise from the lips of the one who is the Truth? Are we really bringing all things under subjection to that rule or is Jesus guilty here of serious hyperbole? Or is He just wrong?

The hard truth is that however hard we might be working, no matter how diligently we might be training up our children to be warriors in the kingdom, no matter how sacrificially we might be living in order to win the great war between the Seed of the woman and the seed of the Serpent, we are not conquering the world. We do not see the boundaries of the kingdom of God expanding daily. Neither do we see the kingdom expanding if we step back and take a broader view. Even looking from the perspective of centuries or millennia, we still don't see the kingdom growing.

On the other hand, to be fair, we are not watching as His kingdom shrinks. The kingdom of God is not retreating, leaving the frontiers to the barbarians so that the center might hold. We are not moving from defeat to defeat, from retreat to retreat. And finally, we are not locked in a Mexican standoff. We are not, like our enemies, entrenched in such a way that neither army can move forward.

No, the reality is that we are not winning, losing, or tied. The reality is that the battle is over, that we have already won. It is not that the kingdom of Jesus Christ is not expanding because the Serpent is thwarting its growth. Instead, it is not growing because its boundaries already encompass all of reality. Jesus rules already in heaven and earth. He already has overcome the world. He does not call us to win this war. He calls us to rest in His peace.

The question we are left with is a simple one: Will we believe Him or not? There is no doubt about what He is saying. When Jesus says, "Take heart; I have overcome the world," we can't wiggle out from under the plain meaning. We cannot go back to the original Greek and turn this promise into something else. The promise is there, like a gauntlet thrown down before us by our Savior and King. The same Savior who makes this challenge to us, the Savior who already has overcome the world, is the one who made the world. While we are called to see our lives in light of the battle between the seed of the Serpent and the Seed of the woman, from another perspective, the battle is all for show.

OUTWITTED AT THE COSMIC CHESSBOARD

The Devil, after all, is God's Devil. He made him. He has ordained all that the Devil does. To understand the nature of the battle, think of it as a chess match. Now imagine that the Devil makes his every move because Jesus wants him to make it. Given that God the Father has ordained all this, what has now changed? God the Transcendent has planned this victory. Jesus the

Imminent has now brought the game forward to the point where He alone moves the pieces on the board, for both teams.

If we think of death as an enemy, if we see it as the queen on the Devil's side of the chess board, we still must remember that when it takes out one of our pawns, it does so precisely because that is the wish of Jesus. When that pawn is His, it enters into eternity in paradise. Even when we lose, we win. Jesus not only has overcome the world, He even now has death on a leash. He has already won.

Our calling, in light of this glorious promise, is to be of good cheer, to take courage. We are set free from the fear of the world. That makes us free indeed. Free from this fear, we are made then more than conquerors. We are empowered to go forth into the war with boldness. The enemy's minions seek to control us through our fears. But now, because we know that Jesus already has overcome the world, their slings and arrows are quenched as we march forward. Our opponents may hiss and spit. They may hurl accusations against us, saying that we are narrow, judgmental, and hypocritical. We must simply shrug and battle on.

We will be free when we believe this promise from Jesus our Lord. But we will believe this when we are free. Earlier, we looked at God's promise that, as we delight ourselves in Him, He will give us the desires of our heart. We noted there that when we delight in Him, He will be the desire of our heart. And He will be, in turn, our exceedingly great reward. In like manner, if our single desire, our great passion, is to see the victory, to see the Seed of the woman destroy the Serpent and his seed, then here too we see the desires of our heart. If, instead, our lives are caught up in our own petty concerns, if we are looking to get ahead ourselves rather than to see Christ conquer, if we are consumed with worries about being well liked, then we are still slaves.

How can you tell where you fall? Of course, we all confess with our lips that our sole desire is to see the Lord triumph. But how can we tell whether our hearts are in line with our lips? It is not at all difficult. When we fear, when we grumble, when we complain, we show forth what is in our hearts. We expose our sin.

When we do not rejoice, we are guilty of one of two errors. First, when we complain, we demonstrate our conviction that Jesus' plan isn't the best plan. On more than one occasion, I've challenged complaints that were made in my direction and I've heard something troubling. "Oh," the complainer explains, "I'm not complaining against *you*. It's the situation I'm complaining about." This is far worse. I explain that we cannot complain against the situation, but only against the one who brought the situation to pass. Ultimately that person is always the same Jesus who controls all things, who has already overcome the world.

Second, when we complain, we demonstrate our disbelief that Jesus has in fact overcome the world. That is, when we grumble, we may be suggesting that we know Jesus is doing His best to solve this situation, but He is not quite up to the task. He has enemies who thwart His will, enemies He has yet to conquer. Perhaps one day, sometime in the future, He will overcome the world. We will just have to wait. We, in short, make Jesus out to be not only a weakling but a liar. He said that He has overcome the world. He is the Word. He is truth incarnate. He does not have the capacity to lie, though we yet have the capacity to not believe Him.

What do we do about our unbelief? The same thing we do with all ours sins, which are, in the end, unbelief. We repent and believe the gospel. When we grumble, and we all do, we must turn from our grumbling and cry out for His mercy. Then we must believe that when we confess our sins, He is faithful and just to forgive us our sins and to cleanse us from all unrighteousness. No enemy can stop Him from forgiving us, for He already has overcome the world. No enemy can stop Him from cleansing us from all unrighteousness, for He already has overcome the world. So let us believe, and let us be of good cheer.

CHAPTER ELEVEN

THE GOOD WORK SHALL BE COMPLETED

PHILIPPIANS 1:6

There are precious few things more disconcerting, more discouraging, than sin. We mourn with those who mourn when calamity strikes a people. Our hearts are touched by the pathos of illness. But it is the ugliness of sin that leads us into despair.

We can tell we've entered into this valley when we fall to the temptation to forget our humanity. That is, we hear a news report of this criminal atrocity or that, and we jump to one of two gratuitous conclusions. A serial killer is captured and we somehow feel safer, affirming, "That guy must be crazy." Or a neighbor is caught with perverted pictures of one sort or another and we conclude, "He must be some kind of a monster."

The sad truth is this. It does not take a madman to commit mass murder. An ordinary man is quite capable. It does not take a monster to destroy the innocence of children. Any man has that capacity. By suggesting that those who commit these kinds of sins are of a different nature than the rest of us, we lie ourselves into false comfort. They are people just like us, and no matter how heinous the sin, there is none about which we ought not to pray with sincere gratitude, "There but for the grace of God go I." Sin is not something out there, making headlines. It is something in here, shaping our thoughts and feelings, driving our speaking and our doing.

The "ourness" of sin is not merely human, either. That is, we cannot merely confess that humans can sin grievously but our close kin are not so susceptible. In my theological circles, we tend to fall victim to this way of thinking because we are strangely proud. The school of thought I hail from begins by affirming that all people are by nature totally depraved. One would think, given that affirmation, that we would have earned a reputation for humility. But we escape the sound conclusion of our sound conviction by seeing depravity as something that afflicts other people from other schools of thought. We think affirming total depravity is some sort of cure for total depravity. But we sin just like everyone else.

Due in large part to the visibility of my father in these theological circles, I have had the privilege of getting to know some of the most brilliant thinkers, some of the most influential pastors, some of the leading lights. I don't know the flashy television preachers. I don't know the leaders in the prosperity gospel movement. I know the Reformed guys, the Calvinists, scholars, pastors, church planters, writers. And what I have found there is sound theology, proud hearts, and, far too often, sexual infidelity.

Sin, however, comes in all shapes and sizes. It need not take the form of sensational crimes. It need not take the shape of scandal. It is ugly enough in the very ordinary forms we face every day. If and when we are honest, we are immediately confronted with the ugly image of our souls. When we look around our homes, we see the legacy of our sins. And if we should ever forget, the Serpent is there to remind us.

When our image of the Devil is that of some sort of über-tempter, we miss his subtlety. To be sure, the Devil does delight to tempt us. But more than anything he delights to tempt us to not believe God. The Greek root for the name *Satan* carries the idea that he is the accuser. Rather than wanting us to forget the truth that we are sinners, he wants us to be all too familiar with the reality of our sin. What he wants us to forget is God's grace. He wants us to believe that our sins are too big for God to forgive, that we are beyond forgiveness. Barring that, he would like us to see our sins not as too big to be forgiven but as evidence that there is no God to forgive us at all. "If," he whispers in our ears, "there is a God, how can we possibly explain the scope and scale of our sin? Surely if there were a God we would be making much faster progress in putting to death the deeds of our flesh."

Pastors here face a double temptation. Because we are most aware of our sins, we face the same temptation as our sheep. We, too, buy into the old canard that because of our role we ought to be even further along in our sanctification. That is, we see our sins and, believing that we ought to be better than lay Christians, fall into despair. (Of course, we have sufficient sin for the same despair even before we buy into this notion that we're supposed to be better than others.) But pastors see far more than just their sin. Our calling is to lead the flock to greener pastures. Our goal is to see the sheep under our care mature in faith, to bear much of the fruit of the Spirit. Though we do not see the sins of the sheep as immediately as we see our own, we do see those sins. And that is where we face the double whammy. Our understanding of our effectiveness is tightly wound up in the obedience of the sheep. So the Devil whispers in our ears that we are ineffective as undershepherds. He wants us to reason that if God were real, He would bear more fruit among the sheep under our care. He accuses us for our corporate failures. Sin, in other words, even before we get to the direct consequences of particular sins, bears this noxious fruit—it discourages our souls, making us grow weary in doing good and causing us to doubt the goodness of God and His power in our lives.

A TITANIC INTELLECT
AND A LION-SIZED HEART

At least one pastor faced the same kinds of troubles. The apostle Paul did not inherit healthy and thriving flocks that had matured under the care of those who had gone before him. Instead, Paul was a church planter, and one well acquainted with both his sins and the sins of those under his care. We ought to remember Paul's profound sense of his sin. Here was a man whose titanic intellect was excelled only by his lion-sized heart. Paul wasn't merely a great scholar, he was a scholar of the Word of God. This same Word so inflamed his heart that he was able to suffer faithfully for the church. We know the stories, the threats to his life, the beatings, the imprisonments, the rejection, all that he went through for the sake of the gospel. Yet he declared that he would gladly pour out his life for the saints under his care. One would think, given the powerful way in which he was equipped by God, that Paul would have been a prime target for one of the Devil's favorite temptations—pride. Don't you think the Devil must have been there all along the way, whispering in his ear: "Paul, you're so brilliant. Why, without you the Christians would look like a bunch of intellectual lightweights. And your bravery. Mercy, you are something else." But Paul did not see himself this way. Paul had a different way of remembering who he was. Paul described himself as the chief of sinners (1 Tim. 1:15).

Paul's awareness of sin, however, did not end with himself. He was in turn acutely aware of the sins of the saints to whom he gave oversight. We know that he knew the sins of his sheep precisely because he spent so much time writing about them. We need to remember that, by and large, Paul's epistles are not merely occasional letters, wherein he wanted only to express his love to churches he had left behind. Many of Paul's letters have very specific purposes. The apostle wasn't just a church planter and a tentmaker. He was, in a manner of speaking, a fireman. His letters were sent in order to put out sundry fires that had come to the respective churches.

One of those letters, 1 Corinthians, has provided a strange sense of comfort to me over the years. I often read this letter when I find myself tempted to despair over the state of the modern church. Now there was a church that was a mess. It was beset with worldliness, pride, sexual immorality, drunkenness, and schism. Paul rebuked the church for accepting sins that would turn the stomachs of even their heathen neighbors. Paul pulled no punches in this epistle. But he did address his missive to "the church of God that is in Corinth, to those sanctified in Christ Jesus, called to be saints together with all those who in every place call upon the name of our Lord Jesus Christ" (1:2). In like manner, in his letter to the church at Galatia, Paul declares, "O foolish Galatians! Who has bewitched you?" (3:1a, highlighting the scope of their sin) but he concludes the letter by saying, "The grace of our Lord Jesus Christ be with your spirit, brothers. Amen" (6:18). In each instance, he looked squarely into the face of grave sin, but wrote to these sinners with confidence that they were believers, saints.

This is our collective problem—we are a body of sinners. What unites us is our confession of sin, but we are called to good works. We are indeed sinners saved by grace, but we are supposed to be transformed by the renewing of our minds. Before we were made new, we were at peace. We sinned, and sinned freely. In Christ, we do not suddenly desire only the good, putting temptation behind us. Now we are at war. Now we have an old man and a new man waging war within us. The battle between our flesh and His Spirit is raging. This is true of us as individuals and true of us corporately. How, then, are we to understand who and what we are? Where do we draw our lines?

Paul, in that same letter to the Galatians, highlights two competing principles. He lists for us the works of the flesh—sexual immorality, impurity, sensuality, idolatry, sorcery, enmity, strife, jealousy, fits of anger, rivalries, dissensions, divisions, envy, drunkenness, orgies, and things like these. This we can accept. But Paul puts these sins in a frightening context: "I warn you, as I warned you before, that those who do such things will not inherit the kingdom of God" (5:19–21). It's one thing to discourage this kind of behavior. It's another altogether to note that those who practice these things will not inherit the kingdom of God. How, then, given our constant struggles with sin, are we to understand not just our standing before God but that of the broader church? How do we avoid, on the one hand, diminishing the law of God, making it something safe and attainable, and on the other hand, falling into a despair that suggests that you and I are the only ones who will make it into the kingdom, and I'm beginning to have my doubts about you? In other words, how do we avoid the despair that dares to wonder, "Who, then, can be saved?" We escape this depth of discouragement by believing the promises of God and by trusting in His sovereign power.

Consider how Paul writes to the church at Philippi. He ends up encouraging the members there to be joyful, humble, faithful, and gracious. But he begins with his own grace, opening his letter with these encouraging words: "I thank my God in all my remembrance of you, always in every prayer of mine for you all making my prayer with joy, because of your partnership in the gospel from the first day until now" (1:3–5). That, friends, is how to speak to a congregation.

"SIR, WE WOULD SEE JESUS"

The Puritans suffer from an undeserved reputation. We tend to think of them as a rather sour group. One reason for this is their strict understanding on how worship should take place. They held a strong view that only those things with explicit warrant in Scripture were permitted in worship. Their church buildings were plain and functional, their singing unaccompanied. There was one place, however, where they were happily inconsistent. Though there is no explicit biblical warrant to do so, many Puritan pulpits had words etched on them, facing not the congregation but the preacher: "Sir, we would see Jesus" (John 12:21, KJV). These words were spoken by some Greeks who came to see Jesus. That the Gentiles were coming was, it seems, the signal to Jesus that His hour had come. The Puritans etched this phrase in their pulpits, however, as a reminder about the nature of preaching. The goal, the preacher must remember, is to show forth Jesus. They reminded themselves thus that preaching wasn't about them but about Jesus.

The Puritans were wise to etch these words on their pulpits. Pastors in our day would be wise in turn to etch in their prayer closets Paul's words of blessing on the Philippian church. We who serve as undershepherds need that love for the brethren, that gratitude for the grace of God, that sense of shared mission that Paul exhibits here.

At the church where I serve, all the children—and there are many—worship with the adults each Lord's Day. We have no nursery and no children's church. That means that we have more noise than some are used to. Babies still cry, toddlers still whine. This, however, is not something that distracts me when I am preaching. I suffer from a different distraction. Often it is related to the little children, but sometimes it comes from the parents. My biggest distraction when I am preaching at the church where I serve is the church where I serve. I find myself looking out at the sheep placed under my care, and instead of thinking about the food with which I am supposed to be feeding them, I am thinking about how good God has been to us to bring us together. I'm thinking how wonderful it is that this family or that family is a part of this body, about how grand it is that Eilidh and Tirza and Daniel and Bliss and Caroline and D.J. are knit together with me and my family. I stand behind the pulpit and behold the glory of the body of Christ, and so I lose my place through rejoicing that I have found my place.

On the other hand, as joyful and grateful as I might be each Lord's Day morning, I find myself too often caught up in worry on Sunday evenings, and every other evening. As grateful as I am for what God has done with our little congregation, I am still given to worry about what might be around the bend. I know enough church history, and enough Bible history, to know that what follows blessing is usually the forgetting of the source of that blessing. Next, the Source of the blessing sends judgment as a means to the end of repentance. When that repentance is forthcoming, God forgives, rescues from judgment, and restores. But we all naturally want to remain in that initial place of blessing. And we all, touching our fallen nature, forget to give thanks.

In the context of the church, this kind of failure and judgment almost always comes in a peculiar form. God does not usually burn down the building in which we worship. He does not usually, in our day, send a plague of some sort into the congregation. Locusts do not come and destroy all our crops. More often than not, the judgment comes in the form of broken relationships. Gossip enters the church. Cliques begin to form. Sensitivities are heightened and we no longer practice a judgment of charity toward each other. Soon, secret committees are formed, contacts are made with outside interest groups, and (in our day) blog posts are written and Web sites created. In the end, churches are destroyed. All because we did not give thanks.

Paul, however, does give thanks. He thanks God with every remembrance of the saints at Philippi. He gives thanks wisely, because the same God who brought together those saints is the sovereign God who would, if it were His design, send them through troubles. Paul understands that even when we fall into the pattern of receiving blessing, failing to give thanks, and falling into judgment, that such judgment is itself gracious, a gift of God calling us to remember to give thanks. God always does good for His people, which leads us to God's promise: "And I am sure of this, that he who began a good work in you will bring it to completion at the day of Christ Jesus" (1:6).

Sadly, people in my theological tradition see this verse as a proof text for the doctrine of perseverance of the saints. Please understand that I believe, since this is my theological tradition, in that doctrine. It holds that all those

who have been genuinely remade, all those who have been called according to God's purpose, all those who have been given the gift of faith, who
repent of their sins and look to the finished work of Christ on their behalf,
despite whatever ebbs and flows they might go through during their lives,
will be redeemed in the end. The doctrine holds that those who believe unto
salvation will believe unto salvation always. One could even argue that this
concept is contained within this text. But I don't believe Paul wrote these
words to the believers at Philippi because they were in danger of believing
that a person could lose his salvation. He wrote them to encourage the saints
with the knowledge that they will grow in grace and wisdom. He wrote them
to encourage them to not despair because of the ongoing reality of their sin.

The text, as we can tell from what follows, is a promise with respect to
our sanctification: "For God is my witness, how I yearn for you all with the
affection of Christ Jesus. And it is my prayer that your love may abound more
and more, with knowledge and all discernment, so that you may approve
what is excellent, and so be pure and blameless for the day of Christ, filled
with the fruit of righteousness that comes through Jesus Christ, to the glory
and praise of God" (vv. 8–11).

GROWTH THAT NEVER CEASES

God is about the business, and will continue to be about the business, of
helping us to grow in grace for all of our lives. He has not merely redeemed
us but is at work in us. Or, to remember a promise we looked at earlier, He
is not only faithful and just to forgive us our sins, He is likewise faithful and
just to cleanse us from all unrighteousness. Were we pious enough to despair
where we ought, over our sins rather than our circumstances, we would be
pious enough to rest in this glorious promise.

There is, in addition to the accusations of the Serpent, another reason
why it is all too easy for us to lose sight of this reality. Even apart from his

constant harping on our sins, there is a terribly natural reason we can grow discouraged, a strange irony to our sanctification that makes our sanctification too easy to miss. Before we are born again, we are generally unaware of any concept of the scope and the depth of our sin. God the Holy Spirit, when He quickens us, convicts us of our sin. But in His grace, He does not show us our sin all at once. At this stage, we are not ready to see all our sin. As we begin in His power, however, to put sin behind us, that sanctification actually causes us to see more of our sin. To put it more clearly, the less we sin, the more we see our sin. The more pious we become, we more we realize how impious we are. The farther away we get from our sins, the bigger they seem.

The solution to this dilemma is to remember God's sovereign grace, to remember the goodness and the power of His promises. It is true enough that each of us has light years to go in putting our sin behind us. But we are in the hands of the one who created space, who spoke light into existence, and who is the Lord of years. Of course, we would despair if we had to walk this journey on our own. But we don't. The one who walks with us is more than capable of getting us where we are going. How hard would it be, after all, for God to sanctify you completely this very moment? He does it every day for many of His saints. We call the process death. He calls the process glorification. As long as we live, however, we move toward that goal inexorably, at the pace that He has sovereignly determined.

We must be careful, of course, not to excuse our sins by pointing to His sovereignty. You cannot rightly say, "Well, I'll stop robbing banks as soon as God gets around to sanctifying me enough." This is Romans 9 territory, the temptation to argue, on the basis of His sovereignty (which Paul so eloquently affirms in both chapters 8 and 9 of Romans), that we cannot possibly be held accountable for our sins. Paul sums up the argument (and the response) this way: "You will say to me then, 'Why does he still find fault? For who can resist his will?' But who are you, O man, to answer back to God? Will what is molded say to its molder, 'Why have you made me like this?' Has the potter no right over the clay, to make out of the same lump one vessel for honored use and another for dishonorable use?" (Rom. 9:19–21). God will not hear these arguments, and they are made, in the end, only by those lumps of clay set aside for dishonorable use.

The promise to us, however, is not merely that we will be molded into something that is fit for an honorable use. The promise we have received is that this same Potter will remold us and reshape us, that He will remove from us every blot and every impurity, making us to fully reflect the very glory of His Son. His is the glory in our glorification. We ought to sorrow over our sins, but not as those who are without hope. For even those sins that yet remain with us remain because of His sovereign plan, because He is glorified in sanctifying us slowly.

This promise in turn turns back on another promise we looked at, that if we delight ourselves in the Lord, then He will give us the desires of our heart (Ps. 37:4). We would be wise to remember that, in the end, sanctification is not about committing this sin or that with less frequency. It is not about committing fewer sins or smaller sins. It is instead about drawing nearer to God.

Even our remaining sin, then, is a means to this end. Just as I delight when my children run to me rather than away from me when they fall into sin, so our heavenly Father delights when we run to Him in repentance, when we draw near to Him as the solution for our sins. He uses the means of grace in our lives. He uses the remnants of the old man in our lives. He uses everything in the fulfillment of this promise, that what He has begun in us He will carry through to the end, to the day of Christ Jesus. This is how our heavenly Father loves us.

CHAPTER TWELVE

WE SHALL
BE LIKE HIM

1 JOHN 3:2

My goal in writing this book has been abundantly simple. Each word is followed by the next with the plain hope in mind that every reader, as well as the writer, will walk away from the book believing God more. I want us to shake off the cobwebs of unbelief, stumbling blocks to our faith put there by the world, the Devil, and our flesh. I want all of us to reply "amen" to every promise that God has made to us, and for those amens to come from the very centers of our beings. Of course we believe that God speaks truthfully. But do we *really* believe it? Does our belief shape our lives? Is that belief something we tell ourselves or is it something others can see in us? Are our lives characterized by the joy that must naturally flow from entering into the fullness of the grace of God?

Raw unbelief is not the only victory the Serpent can win when his forked tongue spews out his lies. Even when we, especially inside the church, do not believe his lies, we often allow those lies to set the agenda for our thinking. Rather than moving forward in faith, we live in reaction to lies.

Consider for a moment the folly of evolution. Imagine a pair of demonic scientists from the Devil's research-and-development department meeting with his infernal lowness. They tell him that they have come up with a bogus theory about the origin of man. They explain that everything began with nothing, which then exploded into everything. Time, energy, space, and chance got mixed together in a bowl, and out popped an amoeba. It studied hard and eventually became a fish. The fish crawled out on dry land, but instead of dying there, it progressed. Eventually, man appeared. The Serpent, in disgust, explains that only the most foolish of fools would ever fall for that. He tells his subordinates that they already control the fools, that the victory won't be won by confusing their own soldiers. The scientists hang their heads and, with their tails between their legs, begin to exit the office. The Serpent asks: "Where do you think you're going? Just because only an idiot would believe this tripe doesn't mean it won't prove useful."

When we rightly reject evolution as a doctrine, we can still get tripped up by allowing it to establish our agenda. The first two chapters of Genesis tell us how God created the world. These chapters are, like all of God's Word, true in all that they teach. But neither Moses nor the Holy Spirit sat down to pen these words millennia ago for the purpose of refuting Darwinism. Their goal was so much higher. The Devil wins when we miss the glory of the story of creation by treating it merely as a set of proof texts with which to defeat the forces of Darwinism.

Of course, we can make the same kind of mistake on a far broader scale. While doing the necessary and valuable work of defending the inerrancy of the Bible, we can miss the actual content of the Bible. In fact, the Devil is delighted when we spend our time and energy defending the Bible, as long as we do not get around to actually reading the Bible. We ought to believe that the Bible does not err in all that it teaches. We also ought to believe all that it teaches. We won't know what the Bible teaches if all our energy is spent on defending the truthfulness of what it teaches.

THE TWO DRIVING SOLAS

It may well be that, still more broadly, we have lost the Reformation because we have been fighting for the Reformation. While the Reformation is rightly remembered for its five *solas*, five critical rallying cries of theological wisdom—*sola Scriptura*, Scripture alone; *sola fide*, faith alone; *sola gratia*, grace alone; *solo Christo*, Christ alone; and *soli Deo gloria*, to God alone the glory—it was the first two that actually drove the Reformation. Martin Luther wisely affirmed throughout the Reformation that the Bible alone had the authority to bind a man's conscience. Indeed, when Luther was on trial for his life, he refused to recant his teaching, saying: "My conscience is captive to the Word of God. Here I stand, I can do no other." When he walked out of that trial, however, he did not run off to write learned treatises on *sola Scriptura*. Instead, he translated the Bible into German so that the people could actually have the Scriptures to believe.

The second driving *sola* of the Reformation was *sola fide*, faith alone. Here Luther argued, again wisely and biblically, that we have peace with God when the atoning work of Christ becomes ours, and that it becomes ours not through our cooperation with the grace of God but through faith alone. Our obedience is the fruit of our justification. It is not that God declares us to be just because we become more obedient to His law; it is because He has declared us just that we become more obedient to His law. This issue, now as then, can descend all too easily into some obtuse theological arcana. Here again, a sound and biblical defense is good and necessary. But it seems to me that, in fighting the errors of Rome, we have been so busy defending and defining what it *takes* to be saved that we have virtually forgotten what it *means* to be saved. We have come to believe, sadly, that this is the end goal, to be saved. Too many of us don't even know what we have been saved from. Others think salvation is all about escaping the fires of hell.

In like manner, we do not devote sufficient attention to the question of what we are saved *for*. This, friends, is not just a problem in understanding ourselves, it is a failure to understand the very person and work of Jesus Christ. He did not take on flesh and dwell among us merely so that we could escape the blazing wrath of the Father. Jesus did not walk this earth, ministering among us, just so that we would not burn forever. He did not absorb the wrath of the Father in our stead simply so that we might not taste the torment of hell. He did not walk out of that tomb alive on the third day merely so that we might not suffer. He did ascend to the throne at the right hand of the Father just so that we would not be consumed.

We have looked already at one promise that gets us a bit closer to understanding what Jesus actually accomplished for us. We looked at 1 John 3:1, where we are told that we are not just *called* the children of God, but actually *are* His children. This does not mean, as the Orthodox would argue, that we are turned into little gods, that we partake of the divine essence. But we must not be satisfied in understanding what it doesn't mean. We have to understand and believe what it does mean.

Several years ago, my family went through a time of homelessness. Well, we had a home. It just wasn't ready for us. The nuanced science of selling one house while building another left us for several months depending on relatives and friends for our shelter. I took the occasion to take a kind of excursis in our family worship. It is our usual habit when we gather for family worship to consider a particular text of Scripture. During this time when we couldn't know for sure where our Bibles were, I taught my children through the Apostles' Creed. It didn't take long for us to run smack dab into the doctrine of the Trinity. That is a brain teaser that the greatest minds in the history of the church have not mastered, and I found myself charged with explaining it to my very small children. I asked the children this question: How could the second person of the Trinity, God the Son, be both a Son and God at the same time? Aren't sons always born, and aren't gods always eternal?

I suggested to them that while sons, as a general rule, *are* born, that being born isn't the defining quality of sonship. I told them that part and parcel of sonship is being in submission to one's father. Added to that, sons are heirs of their fathers. We are not little gods. We are not, as the Westminster Shorter Catechism says of God, "infinite, eternal, and unchangeable in . . . being, wisdom, power, holiness, justice, goodness, and truth." But we are heirs, joint heirs with Christ. This is where we find the real glory inherent in the imputation of His righteousness. By the grace of the Father, we receive all things. Because we are in Him, because of His obedience for us, we are seated with Him in the heavenly places (Eph. 2:6). Understand that when Paul tells us we are seated with Him, Paul is not saying that we are with Him and that we are comfortable. He isn't telling us that we don't have to worry about our feet getting sore because we are sitting down. Rather, "seated . . . with him in the heavenly places" speaks of us sitting with Him in seats of authority. We, like Him, sit on thrones, because we rule with Him.

It is because of His obedience, because we are in Him, that we inherit the earth. When Jesus promised in the Sermon on the Mount that the meek would inherit the earth, He wasn't suggesting that some of us are so meek that we will inherit the earth, while the more belligerent citizens of the kingdom will inherit Mars. None of us in ourselves is meek, and neither do we hunger and thirst after righteousness. The qualities listed in the Beatitudes in Matthew 5 are qualities that, rightly understood, have been exhibited only by the perfect man. But all that is His is ours because of our union with Him.

ELEVATING THE IMPORTANCE
OF ESCHATOLOGY

When I was younger, I embraced what is likely the most common eschato-
logical view. Eschatology is the study of last things, and most views within
the evangelical camp are named on the basis of how they understand the mil-
lennium. Premillennialists believe, for instance, that Jesus will return prior
to a thousand-year reign of glory. Amillennialists believe that the millennial
language in Revelation is symbolic, and there will be no golden age. Postmil-
lennialists believe that Jesus will return after a golden age on earth. I was
what we call a panmillennialist. In this view, we don't pretend to know what
will happen, only that it will all "pan out" in the end. I was not interested
in studying eschatology, and so my motto was, "Last things last." In other
words, after we master every other area of theology, then we can get around
to the confusing issues of eschatology.

I have grown older and have come to understand that eschatology matters, and matters a great deal. Now I argue this way—soteriology serves
eschatology. That is, our doctrine of salvation informs our understanding
of the end times. It is not that Jesus came to save our souls, then decided
He needed a place to put us and so came up with the idea of the kingdom.
Instead, it was determined from before all time that Jesus would be King.
We were redeemed that we might be citizens of His kingdom. The new
heavens and the new earth aren't afterthoughts, but were the goal from the
beginning.

To get to our promise, however, we need to remember that not only
does soteriology serve eschatology, but that eschatology serves Christology.
The kingdom does not exist for the subjects. Neither does it exist for itself.
Instead, it exists for the King. All of the Bible, all of history, exists for the
glory of the Son. In Romans 3:26, we are told this elegant truth, that God
sent Jesus to suffer for our sins that God might be both just and justifier. In

like manner, Jesus is not only the one who earns a reward, He is not only the one who gives the reward, but in the end, He is the reward itself.

Having told us in 1 John 3:1 that we are the children of God, John begins slowly to unpack some of what that means. Verse 2 begins: "Beloved, we are God's children now, and what we will be has not yet appeared." John tells us we know what we are, but we don't yet know what we will be. Why do we not yet know? It is not because God is reluctant to reveal such things, but because, "What no eye has seen, nor ear heard, nor the heart of man imagined . . . God has prepared for those who love him" (1 Cor. 2:9). What is in store for us is yet too grand for our little minds to comprehend. Such does not mean, however, that we ought not try to grasp as much of the fullness of the promise as we can.

John goes on to tell us enough to stun us, to shock us, to give us delightful meat to chew on for the rest of our lives. We do not now know what we will be, "but we know that when he appears we shall be like him, because we shall see him as he is" (1 John 3:2b). We will be like Him.

God's promises are astonishing. When God appeared to Abraham and made covenant with him, God made a series of promises. He told Abraham that He would give him a land. He told him that he would have an heir. He promised Abraham that his descendents would be as the stars in the sky and the sand by the sea. God promised that all the nations of the world would be blessed through him. But all of these promises, as glorious as they are, pale in comparison to yet another promise God made to Abraham: "I will be your God."

In like manner, every promise that we have looked at thus far, as grand and glorious as they are, is but a shadow, a reflection, of this one great and final promise. This promise, that we shall be like Him, surpasses them all, dwarfs them all, swallows them all. Jesus, in all His glory, set aside His glory and came and dwelt among us not merely so we could get saved, but so that we would be like Him. His life, His death, His resurrection, His ascension,

His intercession for us even now, all these are working toward the fullness of the kingdom. All of these are working toward the fullness of our kingship. All of these are working toward our being made to be like Him. The glory of the beatific vision, that we shall see Him, is still but a means to an end. The end of that glory is that we will be like Him.

Given that we are given such a glorious promise, why are we left so unmoved by it? Why do we not shudder with joy when we read this promise? Why do we not face every hardship with peace, knowing that we are getting daily closer to that moment when we will be like Him? It is because we do not know His glory. We do not even seek, as much as is possible on this side of the veil, to take in His glory, to behold His beauty.

YAWNING OVER THE GLORY OF CHRIST

My father, who will be remembered for his book on the holiness of God, wisely focused his skills also on the person of the Holy Spirit. His book *The Mystery of the Holy Spirit* did not sell nearly as well as *The Holiness of God*, even though it touched on issues of charismatic gifts and continuing revelation, the juicy kinds of issues evangelicals like to wrestle over. My father, however, also wrote a book on Jesus called *The Glory of Christ*. It contained the same kind of biblical fidelity that the others had, the same felicity of language that is my father's calling card. But the book's sales languished. His publisher, a Christian publisher, explained that books about Jesus do not tend to do well in the Christian market. That's in *the Christian market*.

My best guess to explain this phenomenon is that we Christians think we already have mastered Jesus. We've read through the Gospels. We know that He died for us. What else is there to know? Wouldn't our time be better spent arguing over God's sovereignty and man's free will? Wouldn't it be more profitable to argue about the issue of the day in our theological circles? Jesus is for children and new believers. Mature Christians move on to the heavy stuff.

We're content to think about Jesus as long as necessary to get our souls saved. We're even grateful for His work in bringing this to pass. But when it comes to our lives in the here and now, we have other agendas, other purposes. We want Jesus to save us, but we want to be like this athlete, that theologian, this rock star, or that political figure. Our heroes are people just like us, and they are what we aspire to be. We take in the glory they have on earth and long for it.

Isn't this how we look at our heroes? At first, we are content to watch them be heroic, to take in their mighty deeds and exploits. Then, as time goes on, we dream about one day getting the chance to meet them. If we should be so blessed, we move past wanting to meet our heroes to wanting to be friends with our heroes, to actually know them. What if, however, God promised you far more? What if He said not only that you could see your hero's glory, not only that you could meet your hero, not only that you could become a friend of your hero, but you could actually be like him?

This is how Elisha thought. He had served and loved the great prophet Elijah. He had become his friend. What he longed for, however, was to be like him. As Elijah prepares to be taken up into heaven, he turns to his student, his friend, his disciple Elisha and asks, "Ask what I shall do for you, before I am taken from you." Elisha replies, "Please let there be a double portion of your spirit on me" (2 Kings 2:9). The request is granted.

As we read these stories, one of the reasons it is so important for us to remember that they actually happened is so that we can believe that they can happen again. God may not come to us directly as He did to Solomon and ask what we would like from Him. However, we can show the wisdom of Solomon by praying for wisdom. In like manner, we could show forth the same boldness as Elisha. We, too, can prayerfully ask that God would be pleased to bless us with a double spirit of Elijah. Or, if we have been given wisdom like Solomon, we may ask still more. We might ask with greater boldness, not that God would give us a double portion of the spirit of Elijah, but that He would bless us with a double portion of the spirit of Elisha. It might be that God would be pleased to answer that prayer positively.

What we know for certain, however, is that He has promised to make us like His Son. We will be like Him. And herein is the very power of that glory—we will be like Him precisely because we will see Him as He is. The power is not found in going through this program or that at church. The power is not found in studying up on this doctrine or that. We will not become more like Jesus by learning new things. Instead, it happens as we see Him. We come to understand His glory because we see His glory. And, in turn, we come to better reflect that glory.

How, though, can we see Him? We cannot, before we have died, storm heaven itself to behold His glory. However, He has left Himself a witness. We may not see His soul here on earth. But we can see His body. For He has told us that we the church are His body (see 1 Cor. 12). As we learn to discern His glory within the body, we hasten that day when we will be like Him. When we behold His glory on His bride, we as His bride remove blots and blemishes. As we love His body, we see His glory, and as we see His glory, we show forth His glory. Our calling is to see Him here and now, and to bring together now and eternity.

We see Him also in the Word. It was given to us as a revelation of Him. He is the Word incarnate. The Word we have now, the Bible, is His story. As we read it, all of it (remembering that on the road to Emmaus He taught the disciples all that the Old Testament spoke about Him), we see Him more clearly. His law shows forth His glory, even as His prayers, the Psalms, and His wisdom in the Proverbs show forth His glory. We see Him more clearly when we take our eyes off ourselves. When we die to self, we step that much closer to death in all its fullness. When we die to self, we begin to step through the veil and see Him. When we die to self, we bring together here and eternity.

This is God's promise. We will see Him as He is, and we will be like Him.

This, and not the end of pain and illness, is the glory of eternity. This, and not the destruction of all His enemies, is the glory of eternity. This, and not wings, harps, and clouds, is the glory of eternity. We will be like Him.

I began this chapter suggesting that I have written this book with a single hope, that I in writing it and you in reading it would go away better able to believe the promises of God. He does not need to promise us more, for His promises exceed all that we could imagine. But we can ask that instead of giving us more, He would give us eyes to see, ears to hear, and hearts to believe. If you have come to this point better equipped to believe, do not be too easily satisfied. In this maturing faith, ask for still more faith. In this growing wisdom, wisely ask for more wisdom. In this cleansing of all unrighteousness, righteously ask to be cleansed still more. In this delightful delighting in Him, ask that you might delight in Him still more. In this seeing Him, ask that you might see Him more clearly.

This is where we are going. Nothing is able to stop us. The God who spoke the universe into being cannot speak falsely. He has promised, and so it is sure. Put the book down and give Him thanks. Bask in the depth and the glory of His promises. Ask Him to help you never to forget. Indeed, have this hope fixed in your heart, because, "everyone who thus hopes in him purifies himself as he is pure" (1 John 3:3).

SCRIPTURE INDEX

Genesis
1:28a, 44
3, 102
3:6b, 2
3:15, 2
11, 46

Exodus
20, 66

Joshua
6:1, 29
6:2, 29

2 Kings
2:9, 133

Psalms
23, xvi
37:1–2, 55
37:4, 56, 123
37:7–11, 55

127:1–5, 46
128, xvi, 92

Proverbs
9:10, 33

Isaiah
25:6, 64

Malachi
1:2–3, 68
1:6–8, 69
2:13–14, 69
3:8–9, 70
3:10, 71

Matthew
4:6, 72
5, 129
5:18b, 8
5:21–22a, 45
5:27–28, 45

28:18, 83
28:20, 80

Mark
9:24b, 35, 80
11:14, 81
11:22–24, 80
11:23, 83
14:36b, 35

Luke
18:11b–12, 23
18:13, 24
18:14, 24

John
10:10, 63
12:21, 119
15:18–27, 105
16:1, 104
16:2, 105
16:29–30, 106
16:31–32, 106
16:33, 107

Acts
8:14–24, 37
15, 33

Romans
1:18–20, ix
3:26, 130
7:19, 24, 9
8, 122
8:28, 94
8:29–30, 96
9, 122
9:19–21, 123

1 Corinthians
1:2, 117
2:9, 131
7:5a, 44
12, 134
13:12a, 61

Galatians
3:1a, 117
5:19–21, 118
6:18, 117

Ephesians
2:6, 129
4:11, 6

Philippians
1:3–5, 118
1:6, 120
1:8–11, 120

1 Timothy
1:15, 116

2 Timothy
3:1–4, 4
3:10–13, 5
3:14–15, 5
3:16, 6

Hebrews
1:3, 98
11:1, 102

James
1:1, 33
1:2–4, 39, 95

1:5, 34
1:6, 35
2:10, 70
3:13–18, 36

1 John
1:8, 23
1:9, 13, 26
3:1, 13, 128, 131
3:2a, 15
3:2, 131
3:2b, 131
3:3, 135

ABOUT THE AUTHOR

Dr. R. C. Sproul Jr. planted Saint Peter Presbyterian Church in Southwest Virginia and is the founder, chairman, and teacher of the Highlands Study Center. He graduated from Grove City College in 1986 and Reformed Theological Seminary in 1991, and received his doctor of ministry degree in 2001.

He is the author or editor of a dozen books, the most recent of which are *Bound for Glory, After Darkness, Light: Essays in Honor of R. C. Sproul, Eternity in our Hearts,* and *When You Rise Up: A Covenantal Approach to Homeschooling.* He is a regular columnist for *Tabletalk* and *Homeschooling Today* magazines. Dr. Sproul has ministered in Russia, Myanmar, New Zealand, and Israel.

He is a husband to Denise and homeschooling father to Darby, Campbell, Shannon, Delaney, Erin Claire, Maili, and Reilly.